CAPTAIN COOK'S
FINAL VOYAGE

The Journal of Midshipman
George Gilbert

IN Purſuance of the Directions of the Right Honourable the Lords Commiſſioners of the Admiralty, ſignified to Us by Mr. *Jacksons* Letter of the *14 Nov 1781* We have examined Mr. *George Gilbert* who by Certificate appears to be more than *Twenty Two* Years of Age, and find he has gone to Sea more than *Six* Years in the Ships, and Qualities under-mentioned, Viz.

Ships.	Entry.	Quality.	Diſcharge	Time.			
				Years	M.	W	D.
Conquestador	1 Nov 75	Mid	8 Ape 76		5	2	6
Resolution Noot	9 Apr 76	Able	3 D 78	1	12	3	3
D	4 D 1776	Mid	6 Sep 79	1	5	2	2
Discovery	7 Sep 79	D	21 Oct 80	1	1	2	3
Diligente	22 Oct 80	Able	7 Mar 81	"	4	3	4
Britannia	8 Mar 81	Able	15 D	"	"	1	1
D	16 D	Mid	22 July	"	4	2	3
Duke	23 July	Act. M.	11 Sept "	"	1	3	2
Victory	12 Sep "	D	11 Nov "	"	2	-	5
			for Capt Cert	6	"	2	1

He produceth Journals kept by himſelf in the *Conquestador Journals for the Discovery & Resolution dispenced with* and Certificates from Captains *King Chad, Thompson Gore, Aunt, Howoth* of his Diligence and Sobriety: He can Splice, Knot, Reef a Sail, work a Ship in Sailing, ſhift his Tides, keep a Reckoning of a Ship's Way by Plain Sailing and Mercator; obſerve by Sun or Star, and find the Variation of the Compaſs, and is qualified to do the Duty of an Able Seaman, and Midſhipman. Dated at the Navy-Office the *15 Nov 1781*

[signatures] *Sam Wallis*

George Gilbert's "Passing Certificate", upon completing his apprenticeship and qualifying commission as a naval Lieutenant

CAPTAIN COOK'S
FINAL VOYAGE

The Journal of Midshipman
George Gilbert

Introduced and edited by
CHRISTINE HOLMES

THE UNIVERSITY PRESS OF
HAWAII   HONOLULU

© Caliban Books 1982

Simultaneously published in the
United Kingdom by Caliban Books

The University Press of Hawaii Honolulu

ISBN 0–8248–0787–1

Printed in Great Britain

CONTENTS

Colour Illustrations, Centre Pages

Resolution And *Discovery* In The Ice Near The Arctic Circle (Webber)

Native Dance At Tonga (Webber)

Portrait Of Captain Cook (Dance)

Death Of Captain Cook In Kealakekua Bay, Hawaii (Cleveley)

Queen Charlotte's Sound, New Zealand (Webber.)

Portrait Of Poetua, Tahitian Princess (Webber)

Nootka Sound, Canada (Webber)

[Note: the pictures "Queen Charlotte's Sound" and "Nootka Sound" have inadvertently been transposed.]

PREFACE

This book makes easily available for the first time the narrative written by Midshipman George Gilbert after taking part in Captain Cook's third voyage of Pacific exploration, from 1776 to 1780.

A descendent of his brother Richard, Mr Alban Doran, gave the manuscript to the British Museum in 1912[1]. There are 165 quarto pages in Gilbert's clear and attractive writing, and a few inaccurate biographical notes added by a later hand. These suggest that George Gilbert died of smallpox in 1781, which is certainly wrong – he can be traced in naval records until June, 1783 – but it does seem probable that he died while still a young man, although the date of his death is unknown. This memoir is likely to have been written in the first half of the 1780's.

There is a contemporary, or near-contemporary copy of it in the Dixson Library, Sydney, Australia (DL MS.94). This version of the journal was anonymous, and Miss Bess Cook, Dixson Librarian, has advised that it came to the library with the collection of Sir William Dixson in 1952, and that he obtained it from a Mrs O. Fairfax Taylor. Its provenance before that is uncertain.

Because Cook's third voyage has received much scholarly comment, particularly in the exemplary editions of various officers' journals made by Professor J. C. Beaglehole (who has also published the last few pages only of Gilbert's journal), the

1 BM Add.MS 38530.

footnotes to this narrative have been restricted to those which might help the general reader. For specialists, the text itself will be of interest as another strand of reference to the history of Pacific exploration, and to the achievements of James Cook. Such readers may also be familiar enough with the story of the voyage, and for this reason the outline given here has been made a separate part of the introduction.

Editorial changes to Gilbert's manuscript have been limited to those which give clarity to its form on the printed page. The text has been divided into six chapters, and dates and modern place names set in the Margins. Modern place names have also been inserted into the text, in square brackets, where helpful. The immensely long sentences of the original – Gilbert indulged in very few full stops – have been broken up when this has made for easier understanding. Also eliminated have been a very few thumb-nail size sketches which were added to the text. Only one spelling rationalisation has been made, which is the use of the '-ed' ending throughout for past tense verbs. Gilbert sometimes used this spelling, but also the ' 'd' ending, as in 'boiled' or 'boil'd'.

Mr John Whurr kindly assisted with the maps, and Mr Peter Gathercole, Dr Averil Lysaght, and Mr Keith Holmes offerred advice and help for which I am very grateful.

C.L.H.

INTRODUCTION

i) – *George Gilbert*

Captain James Cook's third voyage of exploration was mounted in search of a geographical chimaera pursued by Englishmen since Elizabethan times: a North-West sea passage through the North American continent from the Pacific to the Atlantic. His previous two voyages in the Pacific Ocean had effectively dispelled another old theory – that of the great southern continent, once thought necessary to balance the land masses of the northern hemisphere. Cook thought the cold northerly search now proposed by the Admiralty such a 'fair prospect' that he had forsaken the comfortable position at Greenwich Naval Hospital awarded him after his second journey, and volunteered to lead it. Parliament voted prize money for whichever crews made the discovery, as an additional incentive to geographical glory.

Cook's 'Secret Instructions' from the Admiralty (on which he himself had advised) required that the west coast of the North American continent, still called by Drake's name of New Albion, be traced northwards, until the search for the North-West passage could begin in earnest, at about Latitude 65° – that is, beyond the straits newly described by the Russian explorer, Bering. The sea here was expected to be ice-free, because it was generally believed that salt water could not freeze. From this point northward they were to search and explore all '. . . such Rivers or Inlets as may appear to be of a considerable extent and pointing towards Hudsons or Baffins Bays.' They took with them the few available maps of the area, incomplete, inaccurate, and inadequate.

A secondary purpose of the voyage was, en route for New Albion, to return to the Society Islands Omai, a young man who had been taken from Tahiti to England in the *Adventure*, the consort vessel of the previous voyage. Omai had been the man for the intellectual hour in London, a Noble Savage, and had enjoyed two years of life as a social lion.

This was the journey on which the *Resolution* and the *Discovery* embarked in 1776, and for which we have George Gilbert's story. Gilbert was a midshipman on the *Resolution*, one of the 'young gentlemen' in training to become commissioned officers. The tasks of midshipmen, like the duration and tenure of their rank, were ill defined, but on Cook's ships they worked very hard. They were not exempt from scraping decks, hauling sails, and manning pumps, and we know that they rowed their captain for hours at a time in the ships' boats. The professional skills they were expected to acquire during this apprenticeship can be seen listed on Gilbert's passing certificate, awarded when he was commissioned a lieutenant a year after his return (p.000).

Cook's three voyages of Pacific exploration kept the young gentlemen away from home and civilisation for three or four years on end, living in crowded berths, existing on a limited diet, and enduring discomfort and danger. Nonetheless, an officer's training under Cook became such a feather in one's cap, and such a highly regarded proving ground, that families used all the influence they could muster to send a son as midshipman on the *Resolution*, the *Adventure*, or the *Discovery*.

For George Gilbert, however, an appointment on the *Resolution* in 1776 can not have been too difficult to achieve. His father, Joseph, had been its master on its previous great Pacific voyage, and had been considered by Cook 'a steady good officer', with sound nautical judgement. Gilbert Island, off the coast of Tierra del Fuego, was named by Cook after him. On the return of the *Resolution* in 1775 Gilbert senior retired to the shore as Master Attendant at the Portsmouth Dockyard. By April of the following year, his son George had joined the ship at Deptford, where it lay under preparation for another Pacific journey. He joined as an able-seaman, and his rank as midshipman was ratified during the voyage.

We may picture George Gilbert if we will, at the outset of the journey he describes here – a young man of about seventeen, arriving alongside the Thames at Deptford in the early spring of 1776, excited and apprehensive. His previous experiences at sea, on the *Conquestador,* provided only a limited comparison with what lay ahead. Perhaps he had been to Portsmouth to farewell his family. Presumably he carried a bag of personal luggage, for the 18th century navy provided a few individual comforts. On board ship, and around nearby taverns, the rough and often reluctant crew were being entered on the ships' books, and more often than not, deserting again – an R for 'Run' beside their names.

We might wish, unrealistically, for a photograph of the ships' company gathering that April, for among Gilbert's fellow midshipmen and officers were several with distinguished careers in the making. On the *Discovery* there was Riou, who was to die at Nelson's side in the Battle of Copenhagen, and whose monument is in St Paul's cathedral, and Vancouver, whose later marine surveys were to finish what this coming voyage left undone. The master on the *Resolution*, replacing Gilbert's father, was a capable but temperamental man also destined for future fame: William Bligh. The first lieutenant was the experienced and practical Virginian, John Gore, embarking on his fourth circumnavigation of the world. He was to have the sad responsibility of bringing the expedition home to England in 1780. The second lieutenant was James King, a gentle and unusually well-educated officer, whom the

Hawaiians persisted in considering Cook's son! In August, 1779, Gilbert was to transfer to the *Discovery* when King became its captain, to continue assisting him with astronomical observations. In 1776 the *Discovery's* captain was Charles Clerke, a veteran of both the previous voyages, and his first lieutenant was James Burney, brother of the diarist, Fanny. Finally, there was Gilbert's 'great Commander'. Cook was the best-known sea captain of his age, honoured and admired by a wide European public, and the object of feelings very close to love, for many who had served under him.

Gilbert's narrative, although written at some time after his return, has such movement and immediacy about it that we may think of it as a journal. It is a remarkably mature and balanced record, for a very young man, of four years of intense and changing experiences. It is mature because only rarely (in Tonga and Tahiti, predictably) does he paint a place or an episode in colours all light, or entirely dark. No predominant interest or frame of mind overshadows all others. This balanced and independent spirit of observation when turned on Cook, for instance, is neither uncritical nor unrealistic. Cook was forty-seven years old when Gilbert joined his ship, and a tired man. He began, at last, to make mistakes, and his hot temper sometimes flared unreasonably. While Gilbert is factual and uncomplaining about the hardships Cook's own crew had sometimes to undergo, the occasional harsh treatment of Pacific islanders is not glossed over. His mild criticisms of Cook's behaviour in Tonga, in Tahiti, and in Hawaii, are fairly worded, and the feelings expressed tally broadly with, for instance, those of his humane and intelligent lieutenant, King. About Omai, too, the language might be strong, but the assesment shrewd: 'I make no doubt but that he will in a short time be plundered of every-thing he has and be forced to return to his former state.' We know from later visitors to the islands that this gloomy prediction was largely correct.

Gilbert's fair judgement is perhaps the strongest impression of his character the pages give us. It is an attractive feature of what may otherwise have been a mundane personality. Nautical details like the weather and the ship's position, or the decaying state of the *Resolution*, usually take first place in the telling of each week's new adventures. No artistic work of his is known, although his father, Joseph, drew not only sound marine charts, but excellent coastal views. Gilbert is at his best when describing a volcanic eruption, or the fishing equipment of a newly-met group of Indians, or the social behaviour of walruses on the northern ice-pack. He is at his weakest on such rare flights of romance as that on the unsullied golden age of Tahiti – perhaps he felt it was a required passage for reporters of the Pacific. While there is dismay and grief at the killing of Cook in Hawaii, the death of the much-admired surgeon, Anderson, and the slow and brave end of warm-spirited Captain Clerke, are merely recorded. The absence of person-alities is frustrating. There are other qualities we find in the records of various different journal-keepers of this voyage that we may miss in Gilbert's pages – such as the humour of Clerke, the philosophy of Anderson, or the passions and high entertainment of assistant-surgeon Samwell. Gilbert's journal has, in fact, less in common with the atmosphere of any of the more sparkling Cook-voyage writers than it has with the solid realities of Cook's own reports. In particular, we are compel-lingly reminded of the 'workmanlike prose' and 'magnificent lack of imagination'[1] of the younger Cook, in his *Endeavour* journal.

At the end of the voyage the *Discovery* was paid off at Woolwich on 21 October, 1780. George Gilbert was an ordinary naval man, and from here on we catch few glimpses of him. A year later he gained his commission, and we know from

---

1 J. C. Beaglehole, ed. *The Journals of Captain James Cook on His Voyages of Discovery*, Vol. I. *The Voyage of the Endeavour, 1768–1771* (Cambridge, 1955) p. cxciii.

a delightful letter written by his former shipmate, Samwell, that month, that Cook's young gentlemen were still in close touch with each other. On board ship in Plymouth Sound, Samwell wrote to a friend '... we find no small satisfaction in talking over the eventful History of our Voyage and are happy beyond measure when any of our old Companions come to see us from other Ships which they do as often as they can; no less than 17 Lieutenants have been made out of our two Ships; We are perhaps somewhat partial to one another, for it is an article of Faith with every one of us that never was such a Collection of fine Lads take us for all in all, got together as there was in the Resolution & Discovery.'[1]

Gilbert was made fifth lieutenant on the warship *Magnificent,* and served with her in the Leeward Islands until 1783. In June of that year he returned to England in the *Magnificent,* was paid-off at Portsmouth, and we lose sight of him.

1 Quoted in J. C. Beaglehole, ed. *The Journals of Captain James Cook on his Voyages of Discovery,* Vol. III. *The Voyage of the Resolution and Discovery, 1776–1780.* (Cambridge, 1967) p. lxxxvii.

ii) – *The Journey*

The ships took their leave of England – first the *Resolution*, in July, 1776, and then the *Discovery* – from Plymouth. Ironically enough, the harbour was busy with ships fitting out to fight rebellious colonists on the East coast of America, while Cook's expedition set out to explore the West.

After the long journey to Capetown, the last point of European contact before entering the Indian and Pacific oceans, the ships paused to restock with food and supplies. On this voyage, as on his others, Cook was to lose not a single man through scurvy, previously so devastating on long sea journeys. Without being able, in the 1770's, to understand the Vitamin C deficiency which causes the disease, Cook correctly believed that it was prevented by the frequent addition of fresh food to the shipboard diet. His preoccupation with obtaining green vegetables, in particular, spread to all his officers, and is a constant note in Gilbert's journal. As well as food and equipment for one hundred and fourteen men for several years, and ships' supplies and smaller boats, Gilbert's list of animals taken aboard the *Resolution* at Capetown is awesome. The plan was to establish breeding stocks of these various animals on suitable Pacific islands, to benefit both the islanders themselves, and later European visitors. The smell and noise of these crowded beasts, their hooves rattling on the decks at every wave, must be squeezed onto our image of life on board. More importantly, their care proved troublesome, and a diversion in mid-Pacific to find them food and water was, after contrary winds, the last straw which caused a serious dislocation in the expedition's timetable.

From the Cape of Good Hope the ships sailed south to inspect the uninhabited islands of Marion, Crozet, and Kerguelen, recently discovered by French explorers. On Kerguelen they spent a bleak Christmas.

The next stop, at the end of January, was in Adventure Bay, on the south side of Tasmania, still mistakenly thought to be part of the Australian mainland. The first meetings between Tasmanians and Europeans took place, and Gilbert's mention of these 'surprised' people, in the 'most perfect state of nature immaginable, is sad in retrospect. In less than a hundred years, this timid race had been exterminated by returning white men.

After a summery passage from here across the Tasman Sea, they arrived in New Zealand at Cook's old anchorage at Ships' Cove in Queen Charlotte Sound. The local Maori inhabitants gave them an uneasy greeting. Between them and their last meeting with Cook lay their massacre of ten of the crew of the *Adventure*, the consort ship of the second voyage, which by then had become separated from the *Resolution*. For Gilbert, like most of his shipmates, the proven ferocity and cannibalism of these people made even their women '. . . capable of exciting but a very faint desire of aquaintance . . .'

When the ships left New Zealand, on February 25, 1777, they were well behind schedule. They still had to return Omai to Tahiti – or whichever of the Society Islands he chose – and had to be as far up the coast of North America as Latitude 65° by June, to catch the brief Arctic summer. Even if they managed an unusually quick passage to Tahiti they were very short of time.

A quick passage, however, depended on favourable winds, and these they did not get. A month later, they were still well to the south-west of Tahiti, and the cattle were alarmingly short of food and water. Two of the Cook Islands, Mangaia and Atiu, were discovered, but a landing to refresh the animals was made impossible by coral reefs and high seas. The wind continued to blow from the East, against them, and by April 6 Cook faced the fact that the season was too far advanced, and he had missed his passage to the North until the following year. Instead of pressing on against unfavourable winds to Tahiti, the ships turned west, to rest and refurbish their supplies in the Tongan Islands. Cook had visited several of these on his previous voyage and given them the name of Friendly, Gilbert writes, '. . . from the disposition of the Natives.'

Here in Tonga they waited out eleven pleasant weeks, to which we owe invaluable ethnographical accounts of a complex Pacific culture at the point of European contact. Both the men and the *Resolution*'s animals enjoyed plentiful fresh food, and several horses and cows were left in the care of Tongan chiefs.

By July 18, it was time to continue on and return Omai home. Perhaps any sorrow the crew felt on departure from this 'delightfull spot' was mitigated by happy anticipation of Tahiti, the best publicised paradise of all the South Pacific.

Beautiful Tahiti did not fail Gilbert, at least. The scenery, the climate, the fruit, were all enchanting, and although the men were a little indolent and effeminate, after the manly and warlike Tongans, the Ladies were 'more elegant and engageing, than can well be conceived'. The people were again, as at Tonga, 'exceeding dexterous at theiving', and Cook also witnessed a human sacrifice. Nonetheless, several crewmen were well enough pleased to try and desert ship, and Gilbert himself produces a rare passage of light-headed romance about a Golden Age.

With the end of the year, however, came the end of the delightful enforced waiting in the South Pacific. The animals were distributed, and Omai set up with house and land on Huahine. Refreshed and restocked, but with 'the greatest regret immaginable', the expedition left the Tahitian islands, and struck a northerly course. For Cook there may have been relief that, belatedly, he was now on his way to the North American coast, but we can guess that most of the crew, with Gilbert, were sure that the pleasures of the voyage were all over, and expected nothing in future '. . . but excess – of cold, – hunger, – and every kind of hardship and distress.' All these things were indeed ahead for them, but only after a most unexpected and fateful interlude.

First there was Christmas, again spent on an uninhabited island, as on the previous year. Instead of Kerguelen's snows, however, the men suffered blistering heat, and instead of penguin and seal meat, they dined on turtle. After a week on Christmas Island they proceeded north, and the men were soon issued with cold-weather clothing, and put on two-thirds allowance of ships' biscuit. Clearly, no further island discoveries were expected. Nonetheless, on January 25, Gilbert writes, 'we discovered an Island at the distance of 10 leagues . . . and a few hours afterwards another to leeward'. In this matter-of-fact way he introduces the northern-most islands of Cook's last great discovery – Hawaii. When people from the islands promptly arrived alongside the ships in canoes the men were surprised to find, so far north of the equator, yet another branch of the widespread Polynesian race. The people looked to Gilbert like Tongans, and spoke like Tahitians, and tried to make as free with the ships' property as either.

Their attitude to Cook, however, was one of the deepest submission. Gilbert's prosaic interpretation of this reverence was that it arose from fear, after the shooting of one of their number by a flustered lieutenant the day before Cook himself first went ashore. It seems probable though, that to fear was added the awe-inspiring belief that Cook was no mere man, but an incarnation of the God Lono, whose season of celebration it then was. When Cook and his great ships appeared over the horizon at exactly the same time the following year (to refresh after ten months in high cold latitudes) the tension heightened.

The spiritual expectations laid on Cook could not possibly be fulfilled, or even understood, and the resulting frustration on the Hawaiian side played its part in the tragedy of Cook's death.

But in February, 1778, as they left the newly-discovered islands after a fortnight's viewing of them, these events lay in the future. The task at hand was to find a North-West passage to the Atlantic Ocean.

They made the American continent at Latitude 45°, on the coast of what is now the state of Oregon. Now the tedious and uncomfortable tracing and mapping of the little-known coast began. Heavy fog and difficult winds made observation hard, and the *Resolution* (which had been very poorly fitted out in the Deptford yards) needed constant work by the carpenters to keep it seaworthy. For four weeks they anchored in Nootka Sound, on the west coast of Vancouver Island. Here they met Indians, whom Gilbert allows to be Ruddy, if not Red, under encrustations of dirt and paint, and of whom he gives an excellent and entertaining description. Indians and Eskimo were also met at the next stopping place, in Prince William Sound – a large strait which raised many false hopes of being an open sea passage. Westward again, Cook Inlet next proved to offer only an illusory way through into the higher latitudes where their search proper could begin.

From here the unexpectedly long sweep of Alaska and the Aleutian Islands carried them far to the south-west. Off one of the Shumagin Islands some Indians delivered them a letter in Russian, and on their return trip here they were to meet a group of Russian fur traders.

Behind the planned timetable once again, it was July 2 before they could pass north through the Aleutian chain into the Bering Sea, at Bristol Bay, and head for Bering Strait. Finally, only about three weeks, August 9 – September 3, were spent beyond the Strait, and above Latitude 65°.

Within a few days they were met by the high, unbreachable,

and unexpected wall of the Arctic ice-pack. On its edge, Gilbert
writes, 'thro' extreme hunger', they killed and ate walruses, 'the
flesh disgustfull as it was'. They tacked backwards and
forwards between the American and Asian coasts – meeting
Chukchi natives on the western side – until at the end of
August, to the crew's relief, Cook decided to abandon the first
season's search. The winter could profitably be spent, he
thought, in what he called the Sandwich Islands, the Hawaiian
group he had visited the previous January.

No North-West passage had been found, but the coast of the
American continent had been delineated from Oregon to the
north-west corner of Alaska, at Icy Cape.

By the end of October, they had tacked down the Bering Sea,
paused yet again for repairs to the *Resolution*, at Unalaska,
and were sailing into warmer latitudes day by day. The
'hazardous and disagreeable season' was over.

On November 26, the first island, Maui, was sighted. All
was not immediate pleasure for the exhausted men, however,
for Cook frustratingly cruised for seven weeks more, just
beyond reach of the tempting shores. Although it was one of the
rare occasions on Cook's ships when discontent simmered
hotly, Gilbert makes no mention of it, and gives instead what
reasons he could deduce for the unpopular policy. Eventually,
the ships needed water, and accordingly, on the large island of
Hawaii, on January 17, 1779, they anchored in Kealakekua
Bay.

In this bay, among rocks on the beach's edge, Cook, and
four marines with him, were killed by local villagers early in the
morning of February 14. It was a sudden and confused affray,
the sequel to several days of misunderstandings, and, as
Gilbert honestly describes, Cook's impetuous temper. Even
better than his fair report of the event itself, is Gilbert's
description of the hours and days which followed it: the grief on
the ships, the passions of Cook's avenging crewmen, the
restraint and intelligence of Captain Clerke, the gruesome

retrieval of parts only of Cook's body, and the gradual resumption of communications with the Hawaiians.

On March 16, under the command of Captain Clerke, now seriously ill with tuberculosis, the ships and their subdued companies left the Hawaiian archipelago. Ahead lay their second season's northern search, to be mounted this time from the Siberian side of the Bering Sea, from the Russian military outpost of Petropavlovsk, in Avacha Bay, on the Kamchatka peninsula. They arrived there in the intense and fierce cold of late April.

The description of this remote Russian outpost, dreary and isolated, and the hospitality they received there, is an unexpectedly interesting part of the journal. The search for the North-West passage, however, proved as futile as in the previous year, and Clerke's ships were foiled and defeated by the same enemy: the impenetrable ice-pack, waiting in silence beyond the narrow northern strait.

Clerke died within sight of Avacha Bay, as they returned again in August, and was buried there beside the village church in a green countryside transformed by summer. Gore took command of the *Resolution,* and Gilbert was transferred to the *Discovery,* under Captain King.

In October 1779, the voyage home began at last. During a remarkably rough passage, '. . . the most disagreeable we had ever experienced . . . with very Severe Squalls, Thunder, Lightening and Rain and an extraordinary high sea', the ships sailed north-east of Japan, which was then closed to all foreign vessels, and north of the Philippine Islands into the European settlement at Macao, near Canton. To hear 'intiligence from Europe', although it brought 'inexpressable joy', was to discover that the small American rebellion was still not put down, and that England was also now at war with France. The decayed *Resolution* and the battered *Discovery* had thus to exchange an anchor for more cannon, and make the long return to England 'in a state of defence, which had never before been an object with us'. For their American commander, Gore, perhaps there were mixed feelings.

After frustrating delays at the very end, when contrary winds held the ships for a month in the Orkney Islands where, although so close to home 'we could get no more intiligence concerning our friends than if we had been at Otaheite', the ships sailed home into the Thames on October 4, 1780. Captain Cook's third voyage had ended.

Chapter One

FROM ENGLAND TO TONGA

In the year 1776 Captain James Cook undertook his third expedition to the South Seas. The purport of his first Voyage was to observe the Transit of Venus at Otaheite [Tahiti] and to determine whether the Country of New Zealand was an Island or a Continent as part of it had only been seen. That of the second was to determine the Existance or Nonexistance of a Southern Continent. And this his third voyage was in search of a NW or SE passage to the East Indies which has so often been sought for without success on this side the continent but never before been attempted by way of the South Seas.

The reward offered for the discovery of either passage was twenty thousand pounds and five thousand pounds to get within a Degree of the North Pole.

The ships fitted out for this expedition were the Resolution and Discovery; the former commanded by Capt Cook was of 500 Tons and pierced for 16 Guns but carried only 12 which were 4 pounders 10 swivels and 112 men; the latter Commanded by Capt Clerke was of 300 Tons and carried eight 4 pounders and swivels and 70 men. Both of them were Merchants before bought into the Service for this purpose, in preference to King's Ships on account of their stowage. They were put upon the establishment of Sloops of War with respect to wages but different in point of Officers, for the Resolution

ARCTI

ASIA

A S I A

EUROPE

Plymouth

AFRICA

INDIAN OCEAN

Macao

Borneo

Table
Bay

AUSTRAL

Cape of Good Hope

Prince Edward
Islands

Tasmani

Kerguelen
Island

Adventure

**COOK'S THIRD VOYAGE
1776-1780**

O C E A N

Bering St.

Cook
Inlet

Prince William Sound

Unalaska

Nootka
Sound

N O R T H

A M E R I C A

Hawaiian
Islands

N O R T H

A T L A N T I C

O C E A N

Christmas
Island

I F I C

Friendly
Islands

O C E A N

S O U T H

Fiji

Cook Is.

A M E R I C A

Society
Islands

aland

Ship Cove

| Ships' tracks 1776-79 |
| Ships' tracks 1779-80 |

had three Lieuts and the Discovery two and all other Officers in proportion. Each had on board a shallop of 30 tons in Frame stowed in the hold with masts, yard sails, and everything necessary for fitting her up, should any accident happen to the ships. Provisions differed very little from those of other King's Ships except having a great quantity of sow'r Krout, wheat, in lieu of oatmeal, Mallasses for butter and cheese, and likewise a great quantity of portable soup. Neither of the Ships were Coppered, it being rarely done at that time but were sheathed and closely filled with nails. We carried with us a Painter[1] to take Drawings of the people and places which were touched at; and an Astronomer on board the Discovery, our 2nd Lieuts acted as such on board the Resolution, with a time keeper onboard each ship made by Kendal on Harrisons principles, and all other kinds of Astronomical Instruments for Settling the situation of places we were going to.

We likewise carried out Omai, a Native of Otaheite, who was brought to England by Capt Furneaux in the Adventure in 1774.

Both ships fitted out at Deptford from thence they went July around to Plymouth where they were joined by Capt Cook. 1776 After a fortnight stay being ready for Sea the Resolution Sailed on the 13th July 1776 leaving the Discovery in the sound; Capt Clerke being detained by privit affairs but had orders to join us at the Cape of Good Hope.

The winds blowing fresh from the westward, we were obliged to turn Down Channel for 3 or 4 days before we weathered Ushant: Stood to the Southwards with a fresh gale crossing the Bay of Biscay, saw a sail of French men of war; we were becalmed 4 or 5 days off Cape Ortigal; a fair wind springing up we continued our Course to the Southwards, and on the 28th of July made the Island of Teneriff (one of the Canaries) and anchored in Santa Cruiz Bay; found here a French ship of 20 guns which had been settling the situation of several Islands in

1 John Webber.

the Atlantic Ocean. The people here who are Spaniards; brought on board grapes, figs and bananoes, in great plenty; we completed our water and took in some wine for the ships use.

After a stay of 3 days, on the 1st August we sailed and stood to the Southward for the Cape de Verde, which we made on the 13th having had pleasant weather and a fair wind most of the passage. Being off the Islands of Bonovista about ten o'clock in the evening having a fresh breeze upon our Quarter; we saw breakers close under our Lee; had just time to haul up wind and weather them. The next day we were becalmed off the Isle of May; and on the 15th having a breeze we made the Island of Iago; looked into the Porto Prazo Bay, where we saw two Dutch East India Ships but finding the Discovery not there we left the Islands and continued our Course to the Southwards for the Cape of Good Hope. *August 1776*

On the 1st of September, we crossed the Equator in Longitude 27° west and the old ceremony of Ducking was performed on those who had not crossed it before. Caught during this passage 15 or 20 puncheons of rain water. We were driven so far to the Westward by the trade winds, as to be within 10 Leagues of Cape St. Augustine in the Brazils; but the weather being very hazy we did not see it. *September 1776*

About 300 Leagues from the Cape we had a hard gale from the westward; which continued till we got into Table Bay; where we anchored on the 18th October after a long passage of 10 weeks from St. Iago. Sent our Observatory and Astronomical Instruments onshore and a Tent for the sailmakers and coopers. Had mutton, greens and sofa bread, served every day to the ships company who were employed here in overhauling our Rigg caulking the ships sides, repairing our sails and casks onshore; taking in provisions, and in stowing. Which is very convenient; provisions of all kinds are exceeding cheap and plentiful here.[1] The town lies at the foot of the Table Mountain and is very large and commodious: At the back of it are very *October 1776* *The Cape of Good Hope*

1 Capetown.

delightfull gardens, which provide vegetables and fruits of every kind in the greatest plenty and perfection. This Bay lies in lat: 33° 55' south and lon: 10° 23' west, is very large and open to the NW and unsafe to lay in with the wind in that quarter.

November
1776
The Discovery did not arrive till the 10th of November having been blown off the coast which obliged us to stay six weeks being much longer than we intended. Took in here a great quantity of Brandy, Biscuit, and Flower.

December
1776
On leaving this place which was on the 1st of December 1776 we had onboard as much provisions as the ship could possibly store, which at ⅔ allowance of Bread which we were immediately put to, was sufficient to last us 22 months. We likewise carried with us two Horses, two Mares, three Bulls, four Cows, two Calves, fifteen Goats, 30 Sheep, a peacock and hen, Turkeys, Rabbits, Geese, Ducks and Fowls in great plenty, part of which we brought from England and part took in here for the purpose of distributing them among the Islands we were going to; we had them all onboard of the Resolution, the Discovery being too small to take out any of them.

On the 3rd of December we lost sight of the Land and Stood to the SSE with a fresh gale from the westward; carried away our mizen topmast, made another out of a spar we had onboard. On the 13th made two small Islands discovered by the French in 1772; the interior parts are high, and covered with snow; the
Prince
Edward
Islands
shores are steep and rockey having but little verdure on them, they lie in Lat: 47° South and Longitude 37° East, we gave them the name of Prince Edward's Islands. Passed between them and stood onto the Eastward having fresh gales and very bad weather. On the 24th in the morning the weather being very foggy we saw two small high Islands close to with 3 or 4 low ones between them; they appeared to be entire rocks thinly covered with green moss, we passed them; and stood on to the
Kerguelen
Island
Eastward. In the afternoon saw more land ahead, about 4 o'clock we got in with it, and anchored off the entrance of a Deep Harbour: In the morning weighed and worked up it to

which we gave the name of Christmas; as being that Day. We anchored in about 12 fathom water ½ a mile from the head of it to which the soundings are very regular; the Land here is of a moderate height and almost an entire Rock, without the least signs of fertility. The entrance into this Harbour is about ½ a mile wide from which it runs up about two miles; the Shores on each side are steep and rockey, at the head of it is a black sandy beach with two or three runs of excellent water; above which for ½ a mile up is a black soil with thick moss but no appearance of a plant of any kind.

This place abounds with seals, sea bears, penguins, and various kinds of sea birds, one of which is supposed never to have been met with before; it is nearly all white and about the size of a pidgeon and is very good eating. We staid here three Days during which we completed our water, and killed great numbers of seals, and sea bears for their blubber, to melt into oil for the ships use.[1] We found a bottle with a note in it written in lattin informing us that a french ships commander Mons. Kerguelin had been here in 1772, which was the first discovery of this Island. We inclosed with it a note mentioning our Country, the name of our ship and Commander and the time we were there; and placed the Bottle where we found it. This Harbour lies in Lat: 40° 45′ South and Long: 69° 11′ East. We left it on the 28th and stood to the SE, the Land taking that direction passed deep inlets, forming excellent Harbours; there are Several Small Islands lying off here which are surrounded with sea weed, passed great quantities of it, it extending in some places above a mile from the shore. In the evening we came to an anchor in the entrance of a Deep inlet which we reached with great difficulty, the sea weed being so thick and strong as almost to stop the ship. Sent a boat to examine this Inlet to which we gave the name of Port Palliser. We found it to run up

1 The name of the French explorer, Kerguelen, was not actually on the Latin inscription, but he had been in the vicinity in 1772 and 1774. The bay now bears the name the French gave it; Baie de l'Oiseau.

3 or 4 miles, the shore on each side is steep and bold to, with streams of water falling from the cliffs; it is about ½ a mile wide with several small Islands off the entrance; saw very few penguins here, the land in general is higher than about Christmas harbour. Snow lying in patches upon the Hills. In the morning we sailed and stood to the Eastward the shores continued to have the same barren appearance. On the 30th we past the Eastern extremity from whence it trends to the SW; this part of it is low and level towards the shore with High Hills inland covered with snow. On 31st we lost sight of this land which we called the Island of Desolation. It is about 40 or 50 Leagues in extent and uninhabited being too barren for any Human being to exist upon. We continued our course to the East. Had fresh gale and almost a continued fogg all this passage in which we carried away our foretop mast and got another up the same day.

January 1777

Tasmania

On the 27th of Jan 1777 early in the morning we made the SW Cape of Van Diemans Land; Stood along shore to the SE; this country is very high and covered with wood; the shores are rockey and don't appear to form any Harbours. There are some small Islands and rocks laying off the Southern extremity at some distance from the Land; passed within them and continued our course along shore for Adventure Bay from which we were but a little distance; but were detained by calms 3 or 4 days before we got in this Bay[1]; lies Lat: 43½° South and Long: 147½° East and was named from the Ship that went in there last voyage, on Her going out after having parted with the Resolution. We lay here three days and completed our wood and water both being easy to be got. The Bay is large and open with good anchorage; but the surf which runs upon the beach renders the landing disagreeable. Hauled the sieine and caught great numbers of Elephant fish, which were

1 It was in fact January 26 when the ships anchored in Adventure Bay, Tasmania. The bay was named after the *Resolution*'s consort ship on its previous voyage by its Captain, Furneaux, who discovered it after the two ships had become separated.

very indifferent eating, being but little better than Sharks. The shores round the Bay are low, with sandy beaches, and covered with wood, which had a delightfull appearance; about a mile above the beach there are several Lagoons of fresh water full of excellent fish. We cut a quantity of grass here for the Cattle; the second day 5 or 6 of the natives came down to us none haveing been seen here before, they came without any arms except a stick one of them had in his hand which is the only kind of weapon they are possessed of; they seem much surprized at us, but not in the least afraid, and behaved very quietly. Capt Cook made them a few presents with which they seemed much pleased; Omai to shew them his dexterity fired his musket at which they were very much frightened and immediately run up into the woods, leaving the presents behind them; they returned the next day in a greater number there being 20 or 30 of them; they are the only Indians we met with this voyage that have not got canoes. They are of a dark complexion the men go entirely naked the women either throw the skin of some animal or those of birds sewed together carelessly over their shoulders that being all their clothing. Except the Natives of Terradelfuego [Tierra del Fuego] they are supposed to be the most ignorant race of people existing, being in the most perfect state of nature immaginable without the least signs of art amongst them.

On the 1st of February we sailed and after passing Marias Islands, which lie in sight of the Bay we directed our course to New Zealand, had a fair wind and pleasant weather during the passage. On the 11th we made the western coast of New Zealand opposite Cooks Straits which lie in Lat: 41° South and Long:175° East; they are about 6 or 10 Leagues in breadth and separate the Country into two Islands, which extend from 34½° to 47½° South Lat: being together about the size of Great Britain. We stood into the straits and the next day hauled into Queen Charlotte Sound which are on the South side of them and moored in Ships Cove. We saw several Natives in their Canoes rowing about the sound at a distance being afraid to

February
1777

New
Zealand

come near us but after much persuasion were prevailed upon to
come onboard; which they did with great diffidence[1]; I think
nothing can be a greater proof of their treachery than their
suspecting it in us; they pretended great friendship and were
glad to see Capt. Cook whom they perfectly recollected. We
sent the Observatory and Ships tents onshore with a guard of
Marines for the protection of the People that were employed in
repairing the sails and casks, boiling blubber for oil and boiling
spruce (which grows here in great plenty) for Essence to carry
to Sea with us for brewing beer. Wooding and watering are
both very convenient the Ships laying within a cable length of
shore. Gathered scurvy grass which grows here in great plenty
and had it boiled in our wheat and peas. Caught great quantities
of fish of various kinds with our sieine, likewise purchased
from the Natives for beads, nails, hatchets and one kind in
particular which they call a Mogee is supposed to be the most
delicious fish in the world; it is about the size of a small salmon
and not much unlike in shape and I believe only met with in this
country; a boat was sent every day to different parts of the
sound with 8 or 10 people to cut grass for the cattle; I was in
that party and it was lucky for us that we never met with any of the
Natives for tho we had arms with us yet they might have rushed
from the woods and cut us off, the ships not being able to give
us any assistance. One day when we were at Long Island a
quarrel happened at the ships with the Natives when an old
man came onboard and told Capt Cook that some of his
countrymen had a design upon our boat. At the same time they
saw 3 or 4 large Canoes full of men going over to where the boat
was: sent from the ship manned and armed to bring us
intelligence and see whether any thing had happened. She
arrived in time for we had seen nothing of the Natives but
however we were ordered to come onboard. The next day Capt
Cook made an excursion up the sound with 5 boats and 50 or
60 men well armed to cut grass; we went up about 12 miles and

1 In 1773, since they last saw Cook, they had killed ten of the *Adventure*'s crew.

cut two boat loads. On our return we passed Grass Cove the place where the Adventure's boat crew (consisting of a mate, a midshipman and 8 men) were cut off and eaten upon the spot by the Natives. No place could be more favourable for such intentions, as the wood was so thick that the Natives could approach close to them before they were discovered. We saw 4 or 5 of them, who seeing our numbers were afraid to come near us till we made them to understand we had no intentions to hurt them, we had reason to believe there were a great number of them in the woods as those with us frequently called to them; we returned to the ship that night. What we saw of this Country this voyage was very mountainous and entirely covered with wood, the shores are in general steep and rocky and tho the soil appears to be fertile yet there is no fruit of any kind produced in the whole country; and the only vegetables are scurvy grass, and wild sallery. It being in the midst of summer we found the woods very pleasant in which there are a great variety of birds; and some of them have the most melodious notes I have ever heard, but not in the least beautifull in their plumage. The only sustenance that this country affords are fish and fernroot which serves the Natives for bread; I don't recollect ever seeing any of them have birds, therefore imagine they have no method of catching them; the Dog which is the only quadruped in this Country is very scarce, we may reasonably suppose that the Natives kill them for food, for they are in such a continuous state of hunger that they would eat in the most voracious manner the oil and blubber of the sea bears which we were boiling onshore, likewise candles or anything offered to them. In the most Northern parts of this Country they have a few plantations of sweet potatoes but not one here. We made a present of a boar and sow to one of the chiefs; likewise left two on the Island of Motuara in the sound with an intention of forming a breed of each in the Country but I make no doubt of their being eat immediately after we went away.

These Indians are of a Dark complexion, large, well shaped,

and of a robust constitution. The savageness of their disposi-
tions and horrid barbarity of their customs is fully expressed in
their countenances; which is ferocious and frightful beyond
immagination being much more so than any other Indians we
have seen; this is increased by their daubing their hair and face
over with a mixture which would be nearly resembled by
mixing train oil, red ochre and wood ashes together, which has
a very disagreeable smell; notwithstanding that you must salute
every one you meet, which piece of ceremony is performed by
tutching the tip of their noses together. They are exceedingly
filthy and dirty both in their persons and dress which consists
chiefly of a cloak, made of the fibres of a plant which only
grows here, which they throw over their sholders and bind
round them with a girdle; they have another kind which they
call a Buggee Buggee[1] made of long grass and very thick; this
they wear in rainy weather, looking at some distance like little
hay stacks, they having only part of their head out. The women
are dressed in nearly the same manner and are almost as dirty;
and from their small share of beauty are capable of exciting but
a very faint desire of acquaintance in the breast of an
European. The Northern parts of this Country is very populous,
but hereabouts is not so much so; they live in Tribes which are
independent of each other and governed by their respective
chiefs. They are at perpetual war with one another which is
principally carried on by stratagem and surprize in the night,
they seldom, or never having set battles. Those who are so
unfortunate as to be taken prisoners in those skirmishes are
certain of their fates, which is that of being cut to pieces,
roasted and voraciously devoured by the conquerors, the first
opportunity that they have of assembling together, which may
be in a few hours afterwards; their rejoicing on those horrid
festivals are very great. From whence this barbarous custom
first originated is uncertain, as it is rarely met with even
amongst the most uncivilized Indians. If anything may be

1 The *pakepake,* or flax cloak.

offered in favour of its practice here, is that of extreme Hunger. Their arms are long wooden spears and pattoos[1] which are a foot and an half in length and 3 or 4 inches in breadth, tapering on each side to an edge. They in general are made of stone, some few of bones, these they use when they come to close fight, and you seldom see any of the Indians without them hanging by their sides. They have no knowledge of the bow and arrow here, their houses are about 6 feet in height, 10 in breadth, and 14 in length, and enclosed with closely bound together laths leaving only a small space for a door just big enough for them to creep in on their hands and knees. Their canoes are large and well made and either sails or rows very fast and generally carry about 20 men. Their Tiggie Tiggies[2] or Gods are little Images in an human form cut out of a green stone resembling jasper, with two small pieces of mother of pearl, neatly inlayed to represent the Eyes. They wear these in their Bosoms and pay them great adoration, but few of the Natives are possessed of them they being very scarce, and are a great piece of ingenuity considering they have no Tools of Iron or any other metal amongst them, there being no Ore of any kind in this Country; they seem very assiduous in purchasing our Hatchets their own being only stone. They are the most ingenious people at carving we have met with and the only one that carved in spiral lines; their language nearly agrees with that of Otaheite tho at such a great distance. Two of the Natives went with us as servants to Omai, one whose name was Tio wa-rooah was about 16 years of age and the Son of a Chief that had been killed in some of their skirmishes, the name of the other was Coah who was about 10 years of Age. Having compleated our wood and water and got what little refreshments the place could afford, on the 25th of Feby. we sailed out

1 *Patu,* a spatulate club for hand-to-hand fighting made of polished hard stone, or, more rarely, whalebone. Particularly beautiful and valuable *patu* were made of nephrite.
2 The *Tiki* was not a God, but a precious personal ornament, to be handed down through generations of the same family.

of the sound and on the 27th got through the straits and on the 29th lost sight of the Land. The two Boys cried bitterly for 4 or 5 days upon leaving their Country, tho it was entirely by their own consent, but however in a few days they became well reconciled to us.

Directing our course to the Eastward for Otaheite having a fair wind and pleasant weather, on the 28th March in Lat: 21° South and Long: 200° East we discovered a small Island about 5 miles in extent and entirely surrounded by a reef of corral Rocks; sounded 105 fathoms within a cables length of the Reef. The land is of a moderate height and covered with trees having a moderate height and covered with trees having a very beautifull appearance; I saw several of the Natives running along the beach with long spears in their hands looking at the Ships, and following us as we sailed along shore. Two small canoes with two of them in each came alongside but we could by no means preswade them to come onboard; they reconnoitred us very closely, and with great amazement; they were much like the people of Otaheite (from which this Island is 200 Leagues distance) both in their person, and dress, tho their Language seems to be very different, they wear only a small piece of cloth round their waist this climate requiring nothing more; their canoes were very neatly made and like those of the Friendly Islands; they brought off with them 3 or 4 cocoa nuts and a bunch of green plantains which we purchased with a few small nails. Seeing no possibility of a boat being able to land, we left the Island being greatly dissappointed, as we began to be very short of water and refreshments for the Cattle—

The next day we discovered another Island of the same extent with the same beautifull appearance and likewise entirely surrounded with a reef of coral rocks; sent two boats armed with an Officer inshore to see if it was possible to land which they found impracticable for our boats, but the Natives offered to carry them onshore in their Canoes in which way three of our Gentlemen and Omai landed: they were carried up to the

March 1777

Mangaia, Cook Islands

April 1777

Atiu, Cook Islands

House of the Chief and detained there two hours and were treated with great civility and presented with the fruits of the Island: but before they were suffered to come away, the Natives robbed them of every thing except their clothes and then brought them off to the boat without offering any other kind of violence; Omai met with 5 or 6 of his countrymen who had been driven here by the trade winds; this Island being about 200 Leagues to leeward of Otaheite; one of the Natives wanted to come onboard, he seemed very much afraid, and was glad to get to his canoe again. They brought off to us a hog, some coconuts, and plantains, as presents and desired we would give them in return a dog that they saw and took a fancy for which we did; they seemed much pleased with us and promised to bring more hogs and fruit the next day; but having no time to spare we did not stay for them, but stood for a small low Isle that we saw at about 4 Leagues distance; it is about a mile in   Takutea extent and covered with coconut and palm trees and nearly surrounded with a Reef to leeward of the Island. Sent our boats inshore, which found an opening in the Reef where they landed and brought off a quantity of coconuts and palm cabage. There are no inhabitants here nor any water, which we began to be in want of; therefore we did not stay but stood for Herveys Islands which we made the next day. They are two small Isles joyned   Hervey by a reef and shoal water betwixt them and are together about 3   Island miles in extent; they are exceeding low, and covered with trees, and bushes to the waters edge, having a very beautifull appearance, being regularly planted out into delightfull walks and gardens; sent two boats armed inshore to sound for anchorage found 30 fathoms within two cables of the shore but very rocky. The Natives who were assembled on the beach in great numbers made use of every method to preswade our people to land which they declined. Several of them came alongside in their canoes and ventured onboard the ship; we purchased a few fish of them which was the only thing they brought off; these Indians are of a darker complexion than those of the two Islands we had just left, tho at such a small distance and have something savage in their countenance.

Being now nearly in the parallel of Otaheite and 10° to the Leeward of it, finding the wind to continue steady from the eastward and our water beginning to grow very short, we gave over all thoughts of reaching it; and bore away to the westward for a cluster of Islands discovered by Tasman a Dutch navigator and visited by Capt Cook on his second voyage to which he gave the name of Friendly from the disposition of the Natives. This effectually prevented our going to the west of America to search for a passage this season – as we could not go to the Northward till we had first landed Omai at his Native place and disposed of the cattle we brought with us amongst the Islands.

During this passage which was attended with thunder, lightening and hard rains, we were forced to kill several of our sheep on account of the scarcity of water onboard. We began to distill fresh water from salt by which we procured very little and it was attended with great trouble. In our way we touched at Palmerstones Isle's, which lie in Lat: 18° South and Long: 197° East; they are a cluster of small low ones being in the form of an oval about 2 Leagues in extent and joyned by shoal water and a reef of Coral Rocks which surrounds them. They are entirely covered with Coconut trees, palm trees and bushes appearing very delightfull. We found no inhabitants here; nor any water and the landing was rather diffcult by reason of a surf running upon the Rocks; having no ground fit for anchorage we stood off and on for three days during which we were employed bringing onboard Cocoa nuts with grass and palm cabbage for the cattle; from hence we continued our course to the westward, and past Savage Island [Niue]; which we saw at a distance.

On the 28th of April 1777, we made the Torring Islands; and on the 1st of May came to an anchorage at Anamocka [Nomuka] so called by the Natives, but by Tasman[1] Rotter-

Palmerston
Island

May
1777

1 The Dutch explorer Abel Tasman discovered the Tongan Islands in 1643.

dam. This Island is low and about 6 miles in extent with a Lagoon of flat water in the middle of it; and is in my opinion the most delightfull spot in the world, being covered with a variety of trees and bushes forming the most shady and agreeable walks I ever met with; we moored here in 12 fathoms water, the bottom rather rocky about ½ a mile from a sandy beach. The Natives came onboard in great numbers and behaved in the most Friendly manner being very much rejoiced at seeing the ships again. They brought onboard Hogs, Fowls and fruit in great plenty; which we purchased of them for hatchets, nails and beads, every species of the ships provisions was from this time stopped and we lived intirely upon the productions of the Islands which was very agreeable to us; sent out Tents on shore and the observatories with the Astronomers Instruments for making observations, to regulate our time keeper; had a guard of Marines onshore for their protection; sent the cattle onshore for some refreshments, which they were much in want of, being reduced very low. The Discovery had both her cables cut thro' by the coral rocks, she was lucky enough to get both her anchors again after great trouble; hove our cables in to examine them but found 'em not in the least damaged. Had parties on shore cutting wood and watering from a small pond about a ½ of a mile above the beach which was muddy and brackish and the only water we could get, but the milk of the cocoa nuts in a great measure made up for the badness of it, as they were so plentifull that we seldom drank anything else. As we secured more hogs here than were sufficient for present use, we began to salt pork for to carry to Sea. About a week after we came in a great chief named Feenow[1] arrived here from Tongataboo [Tongatapu] a neighbouring Island; he appeared to be of a superior Rank to those here, who paid Him great respect. He come onboard with Capt Cook who made Him several presents; we fired some great guns, to shew Him the use of them, at which He seemed much surprized, but not in the least

1 Finau Ulukalala.

afraid. This chief informed us of three Islands laying close together, each as large as this, which he said belong to Him; and promised to go with us and show us the way, and to supply the ships with provisions whilest they staid there which he faithfully preformed. Finding supplys beginning to grow short here, on the 14th of May we sailed for the Islands above mentioned; the chief going with us in his canoe passed by two small high Islands, which lie 11 Leagues NNWest of that we left; on one of them is a Vulcano. Having passed several small Islands and reefs, we arrived at those we were in search of; found them to lie 15 Leagues, to the NE of Anamocka we anchored off one of them called Lefooga [Lifuka] a ¼ of a mile off shore. Those three Islands are called Happi [Ha'apai]; each about the extent of that we left; they lie very close to each other, are exceedingly low and covered with trees; and tho' they are in the same cluster with the next of the Islands, yet were never seen before. We found no water upon them but were plentifully supplied by the Natives with provisions. Another Cheif arrived here from Tongataboo named Tawlahow[1] of a still superior Rank to Feenow. He came onboard and desired to know what our business was there and where we came from; Capt Cook perfectly satisfied Him on these points, and made Him several presents with which he seemed much pleased. We entertained them with some fireworks at which they were greatly surprized and delighted particularly with the Sky Rockets. After a stay of 11 days we sailed back to Anamocka, stopped there two days then set sail for Tongataboo or Amsterdam which lies 15 Leagues SSW of it:

Before we could get in with the shore we were obliged to pass over a shoal of Coral Rocks, a league in breadth which extended along the north side of the Island at 5 or 6 miles distance from it; having light airs and calms, we were under the necessity of coming to anchor twice upon it, the ships tutching

Lifuka, Tongan Islands (margin note)

June 1777 (margin note)

---

1 This man was Fatafehi Paulaho, the 36th *Tui Tonga*, and sacred chief of the whole Tongan group.

and breaking off the heads of the Coral as she sailed along; having got clear of it we deepened our water and came to an anchor in a fine bay formed by small Islands and the main Land with good sandy bottom. Moored a cable each way ⅓ of a mile from the shore. Sent our tents and observatory onshore with a party of Marines, likewise our cattle for refreshment. Our employment here was repairing our sails and casks, wooding and watering from a pond in the middle of one of the small Islands near us, which was very thick and brackish. Likewise salting down pork for sea, and trading with the Natives for yams of which we got a great number. This Isle which is by far the largest in the Cluster is about 7 leagues in length and 5 in breadth, is throughout low and level with the same appearance as the others; we observed part of an Eclipse of the Sun here. The two Cheifs mentioned before came with us; and behaved in the most friendly manner immaginable; and supplied the two ships with provision in great plenty; in all their proceeding they showed a Noble generous and disinterested spirit; and tho' their manners were rude and unpolished yet in every action they displayed an elevation of the mind that would do honour to an European in the most distinguished sphere in Life. Played off some fireworks here which were viewed by a numerous assembly with acclamations of admiration and surprize. These Indians are very dexterous at thieving and as they were permitted to come onboard the ships in great numbers, they stole several things from us. This vice which is very pervilent here, Capt Cook punished in a manner rather unbecoming of an European viz: by cutting off their ears; fireing at them with small shot, or ball, as they were swimming or paddling to the shore and suffering the people[2] (as he rowed after them) to beat them with the oars, and stick the boat hook into them where ever they could hit them; one in particular he punished by ordering one of our people to make two cuts upon his arm to the bone one accross the other close below his shoulder; which was

Tongatapu, Tongan Islands

1 i.e. the crew.

an act that I cannot account for any otherways than to have proceeded from a momentary fit of anger as it certainly was not in the least premeditated.

We left here, with the chiefs, a horse and a mare, and a young bull and a Heifer brought from the Cape of Good Hope with which they were much pleased and took great care of them, they had quite recovered their strength during the time they were onshore here; and began to look very well again.

July
1777

Finding supplies begin to grow short, from our having drained this part of the Island of what the Natives could conveniently spare; after a stay of 5 weeks, we sailed for Eaowee [Eua] or Middleburgh which lies about 3 Leagues from the otherside of this Island to the SE; we were obliged to work through a very narrow and intricate passage to the eastward, before we could get clear of the Land. The next day we came to an anchor in English Road;[1] which is quite open to the sea, and a great swell setting in; which made it bad riding.

Eua,
Tongan
Islands

This Island is about 4 Leagues in length 2 in breadth, is high and presents a most beautifull prospect from the sea; but is not so fertile as the others that are low. Found a large rivulet of excellent water which is the only one known at these Islands, but a great surf that breaks upon the shore which is rockey renders the watering very difficult; got onboard but very little for the wind blowing fresh prevents us; got but few supplies here from the Natives who are rather of a savage disposition, differing much from those of Amsterdam. One day when Capt Cook was onshore with a party trading for provisions, having nothing with him but his hanger and a fouling piece that one of the Officers had brought onshore, one of our people separated from the rest and went up about a mile into the Country; where he was met by the Natives who robbed him of everything, then run away and left him naked, they at the same time had a very strong inclination to attack the whole party: Which Capt Cook

1 This name was given to the channel between Tongatapu and Eua by Cook in 1773.

preceiving sent onboard for arms and by a resolute and
undaunted courage prevented. After a stay of 8 days here, and
two months and three weeks at these Islands, on 18th July
1777 we set sail for Otaheite.

These Islands are situated in 20° South Lat: and 185° East
Long: they are very populous, fertile and well cultivated,
producing yams, plantains bananoes, bread fruit and cocoa
nuts, in great plenty, and a few shadocks and sugar cane, all of
which are purchased with nails and beads. Their only
quadrupeds are hogs, dogs and rats: Fowls are very plentifull
here, and of the same kind as in England; their birds of which
they have no great variety are small and cheifly paraquets,
which have the most beautifull plumage I ever saw; but no note.
Bats likewise are frequently met with here.

Besides the Islands I have particularly mentioned, there are
about 30 more small ones interspersed with the Cluster, they
are low and covered with trees and bushes to the waters edge,
appearing very beautifull; there are several reefs running off
from them, some at a considerable distance, which renders
navigation here very intricate and dangerous. The Chiefs
inform us of an Island larger than Amsterdam; to which they
are obliged to pay tribute, and that it lies about 3 days sail to the
westward from hence;[1] it is somewhat surprizing that Capt Cook
did not go in search of it according to His usual practise. His
reasons for not doing it I can't account for; as we certainly had
time while we were lying at Tongotaboo. These people are tall
strong and very active; their complexion is somewhat darker
than that of the Otaheitians, their features are regular and well
formed, their countenances very pleasing; their appearances
manly and war like; and their behaviours, friendly and
agreeable; their clothing is only a small piece of cloth wrapt
round their waists, and is made from the bark of a tree which
they cultivate for that purpose. The cheifs are distinguished by
wearing a greater quantity round them; and of a better quality.

The
Tongan
Group

1 The Tongans described the island groups of Samoa and Fiji.

The women altho' they have something masculine in their appearances yet! their countenances are pleasing, and their disposissions very mild and agreeable; their actions altho' they are innocent enough according to their ideas, yet! are certainly very lacivious, and seem to be intirely unrestrained by custom; their dress likewise consists only of a piece of cloth wrapt round their waist reaching to their knees, in which they are exceeding neat and clean, as well as in their persons, they are always full of mirth and vivacity; and very fond of singing and dancing according to the customs of their country. They are not permitted to eat in the presence of the men. Fish are very scarce here; the Natives catch them with a small sieine net of the same construction as ours but much finer. The time they chuse for fishing, in in a dark night with lights, what few they get are small and indifferent; both men, and women are very fond of the water and used to swim off the ship at some distance. They were much surprised at our cattle and called them Boa ha la hi; which signifies large hogs, having seen nothing of the kind before. We purchased a great quantity of red feathers here, to carry with us to Otaheite, as the natives there are exceedingly fond of them. The plantations at these Islands are neatly fenced round with strong Reeds and in the middle of which the owners generally have their houses, which are neat and of various sizes; the roof is well thatched with reeds, and resembles that of a country cottage, the lower part is of an oval form, supported by several upright pieces of wood and is not above 3 or 4 feet from the ground, raising in the middle to a ridge about 10 feet high; the sides are open all round. This delightfull climate requires no other shelter but that of the Roof to keep the rain and sun from them; the floor is covered with matts which they sit upon having no chairs, nor stools, for that purpose. What few utensils they have are hung up under the roof. In the night when they go to sleep they cover themselves with large pieces of cloth, they have for that use, and place their heads upon a small wooden stool about 5 inches high for a pillow. At all these Islands they go to rest with the sun and raise with Him in the morning. The arms used by these Indians are principally Clubs, made of a hard kind of wood and about 4 feet in length which they manage very dexterously and are likewise very expert at boxing. Their canoes are made of planks cut out with stone hatchets and lashed together exceeding neat, and close, with line made from the rind of cocoanuts; the single ones are from 25 to 30 feet in length and not more than 20 inches in breadth. They lash two pieces of wood across the canoe towards the ends, as outriggers, which reach over one side; to the outer end of these and about three feet distance they lash a piece of wood parallel to the canoe, and nearly its length, and shape but small; which swims upon the surface of the water and prevents the canoe from upsetting the extremities of them are planked over, leaving only about half of the canoe open. They are made very neat and carry from two to six of the Natives who paddle along in them very swiftly; their sailing canoes are too like the others but five times as large, joined parallel to each other at 5 or 6 feet distance by a platform of planks lashed across both; and extending over the outer sides some feet; upon this they step the mast and steady it with guys from different parts of the canoe. They have only one sail which is made of strong matts sewed together and bent to two yards, and is suspended on the mast on the platform; they generally have a hut to keep the sun from them, and to sleep in. These canoes are able to carry 30 or 40 men, but in general have no more aboard but the Family they belong to; who usually have 3 or 4 days provisions with them. They are neater built, sail faster, and are much better navigators than any we saw during the voyage. The two boys that we brought from New Zealand who by this time were very well reconciled to us, were much delighted at these Islands, especially with the fruits which they have no idea of in their own Country. The bread fruit trees, which only grow in the South Seas, is large and spreads like an oak; the fruit is nearly round and about 6 or 7 inches in diameter; it is covered with a thin rind and has a small spongy core in the middle of it; the rest of it is good eating when boiled or roasted, but before that is something like a raw potatoe. It is very dry and insipid and entirely different from anything we have in England. These Indians have no idea of boiling their Victuals, as they have got no vessels that will bear the fire to heat water in. They kill their hogs by beating their heads with a stone; they then burn the hair, and scrape it off clean; and after the entrails are taken out and the hog well washed they dress it whole in the following manner; which by us is called barbacued. They have got a hole in the ground lined with stones; just large enough to hold the Hogs; in this they make a fire and throw into it a number of small stones sufficient to cover the hole, when it is well heated when the loose stones are all red hot they take out the fire, and put 3 or 4 of the hot stones into the inside of the Hog; and wrap it up well with plantain leaves, which are very large being from 3 to 5 feet in length and one in breadth; they then put it into the hole and cover it with the hot stones over which they first throw the hot embers, and then a quantity of dry earth; which keeps the heat in. They let it remain for a certain time, according to its size; till it is sufficiently done. By this method it is not in the least burnt; it is very tender and full of gravy (the plantain leaves keeping it all in) and is in the opinion of every one that had tasted it, much preferable to roasting. This way of cooking them is made use of by all the Indians in the South Seas. We procured sufficient quantity of yams, and pork salted at these Islands to last us to Otaheite to which, we were now going.

We stood to the south, to get out of the trade winds, and in the Lat: of 32° South we met with a hard gail of wind from the westward which lasted two days; the Discovery carried away her main Topmast and sprung the head of her mainmast.

August 1777   In Lat: 23° south and Long: 211° East we discovered an Island[1] about 5 miles in extent, surrounded with a reef of coral rock running off some distance from it; the interior part raising

1 Tubuai, in the Austral Islands.

into two high hummocks; the shore is low and covered with cocoanut trees which had a pleasant appearance, two large single canoes with 8 or 10 of the Natives in each came off within ½ a mile of the ship. We tried all methods to preswade them to come alongside, but without effect; they continued to paddle about near us for upwards of an hour singing and shouting the whole time; they were of a much darker complexion than any Indians we have seen between the Tropics, and from every appearance, of a very savage disposition. The wind being fair we did not stop here but proceeded on to Otaheite from which we were only 100 Leagues distance.

Tubuai

Chapter Two

THE SOCIETY ISLANDS AND THE DISCOVERY OF HAWAII

On the 12th of August 1777 we made the Island of Otaheite which is considerably the largest of a cluster, called by Capt Cook the Society Islands; the next day we came to an anchor in Oai tepeeha Bay [Vaitepiha Bay]; which lies on the North Side of little Otaheite; it is formed on one side by low land and on the other by a reef of coral rocks; there are several rivulets of excellent water emptying themselves here, the interior parts are very hilly, the low land and the Vallies are exceeding fertile and covered with fruit trees and bushes appearing very delightfull The Natives came on board in great numbers; were much rejoiced at our arrival, and seemed to express real pleasure on seeing Capt Cook again, whom they all recolected, this being the third time he had visited them; they were likewise much pleased at seeing Omai again, especially when he told them that he had been in England; they throng round him, and were very eager in asking him questions; but after an hour or two their curiosity subsided, and they seemed to take very little notice of him; which principally proceeded from his stupidity, and his being one of the meanest degree amongst them. He met with his sister here who received him with tears of joy. The

Tahiti, Society Islands

Natives informed us that the Spaniards[1] had been there twice since we were here last; that they came from Lima in South America in two ships much larger than ours; and had been gone only two months. Capt Cook was very sorry to hear this, as fearing that they had impoverished the Island and that we should get but little supplies; but we found every thing in great plenty. The Spaniards had left a wooden house here with two rooms in it, which they had brought with them in frame; the planks being all numbered. The Natives told us that their Capt died here and was buried at the foot of a cross they had set up with this inscription upon it; Christus vincit Carolus imperat: and the year in which they were there. Capt Cook, had put upon the otherside of it, Georgius tertius Rex; and the five different years we were there. By what we can learn from the Natives the Spaniards were very industrious in telling them that we were Pirates; that the English were a nation of very little consequence and that they were much superior to us. The latter the Natives seemed firmly to believe; which I suppose arises from their having larger ships, and their Officers being better dressed which we took but little care about at those places. Notwithstanding these prejudices the Natives confessed that they liked us best; for the Spaniards would not permit them to come onboard their Ships, but always keep them at a great distance whereas we were ever on friendly footing, and had the most intimate connexions with them. We promised ourselves great pleasure in shewing the Natives our cattle, but were much disapointed when we found that they were little surprized at them which we could not conceive the reasons of; till they told us that the Spaniards had left a Bull and a Cow there but that the latter was dead. After a stay of 11 days, having had hard rains, thunder, and lightening, most of the time we set sail for Matavai

1 The *Aguila,* commanded by Don Domingo de Boenechea, came to Tahiti in 1774 from Lima in Peru, and settled two Franciscan monks on the island, with a servant and an interpreter. They were to establish a Christian mission on the island. Boenechea died while in Tahiti, and was buried there in 1775. The mission was a failure, and the friars were taken back to Peru at the end of 1775.

Bay, where we arrived the same day. This Bay lies to the North side of Great Otaheite, to which Little Otaheite is joined by an Isthmus of low land; the Bay is large and open, is well sheltered from the Traid Winds, and has very good anchorage from 12 to 4 fathoms. We moored a cable each way about ½ a mile from the shore. The interior part here is very mountainous, the lowland and vallies are exceeding fertile, being covered with trees of various kinds; and abounds in large rivulets of excellent water. The Natives came onboard in great numbers, amongst whom was O too[1] the King of the Island who expressed great pleasure on the arrival of Capt Cook, who made him several valuable presents. We sent our tents and Observatory onshore with a guard of Marines for their protection; likewise all our casks and sails to be repaired. The Discovery was obliged to get Her mainmast out here, having sprung the head of it, as before mentioned; got it onshore and had new oak cheeks put on it, which made it as servisable as ever.

Struck our yards and topmasts and overhauld all our rigging, which we found in very good order; likewise caulked the ships sides and painted them with varnish of pine. Our other employments here were watering, trading with the Natives for provisions, which we procured in great plenty, and in salting pork for Sea. Found the Bull here that had been left by the Spaniards which was very large and rather wild. The gotes left here by Capt Cook on his last voyage had increased in their number greatly and were in excellent order and very tame. We entertained the Natives with some fireworks with which they were much surprized, and delighted. For which in return they favoured us with a review of their Fleet belonging to three or four of their neighbouring districts; which assembled here on this occasion and consisted of 70 war canoes. These canoes are two large ones about 45 feet in length joined parallel to

1 Tu was not then the 'King of the Island'; no such central authority existed. He was merely the chief of the district around Matavai Bay. After such a good start with European patronage, however, he did eventually become the first King of Tahiti, as Pomare I.

ISLAND GROUPS OF THE CENTRAL PACIFIC

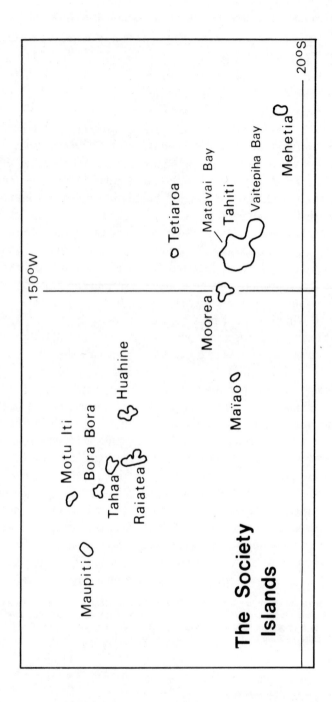

The Society Islands

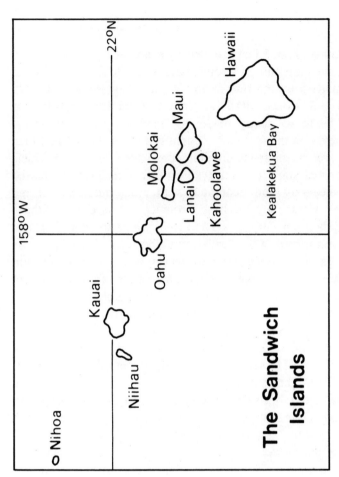

The Sandwich Islands

Nihoa

22°N

158°W

Niihau

Kauai

Oahu

Molokai

Lanai

Maui

Kahoolawe

Hawaii

Kealakekua Bay

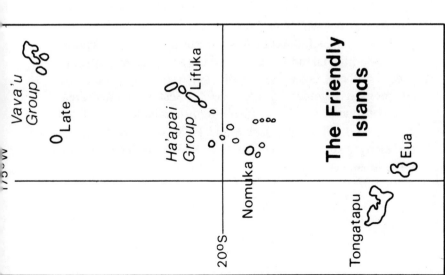

The Friendly Islands

Vava'u Group

Late

Ha'apai Group

Lifuka

Nomuka

20°S

Tongatapu

Eua

each other about 5 feet asunder, by spars lashed across both of them; they are built of strong plank lashed together with small line made from the rind of cocoa nut. They are considerably larger and stronger than those at the Friendly Islands but far from being so neatly made; for they are very heavy and clumsey:– on the fore part of them is a stage about 4 feet high and 8 feet in length and breadth, upon which from 5 to 8 Chiefs or warriors stand to fight, who on this occasion was dressed very elegantly and decorated with great quantities of red feathers which they purchased from us, and used only at those times; their arms are spears and clubs which are placed upright and form a kind of barricade round the stage. The other parts of the canoe contains about 30 rowers, who having nothing but their paddles, bear but a small share of the offensive parts of their engagements. These canoes when all assembled together, with the number of small ones that attend them, and the great crowd of the Natives that attend onshore, made this review very brilliant and warlike. Omai, took this opportunity of appearing on Horseback in a compleat suit of bright armour, studded with brass at which the Natives were much surprized and delighted, but very unfortunately after he had it on about two hours, one of the joints broke, close above the knee, which rendered it useless. He likewise had with him a coat of mail both of which were made him a present of in England.

September 1777   While we were laying here Capt Cook with some of our Gentlemen went a few miles up into the Country to see an human sacrifice which was to be made to their Deity to entreat success in a expedition they were preparing to go upon against a neighbouring Island.[1] These sacrifices are very rare, and only used on these occasions; upon which all the people are summonsed together by their chief priest who after great ceremony and supposed inspiration nominated the fated victim, who is instantly seized and killed upon the spot; the ceremony is afterwards performed with his body. This I am not

1 Eimeo, also called Moorea.

acquainted with; till this voyage we had no idea that this horrid custom was practiced at those Islands, but I firmly believe it prevails more from the power of their priests, and their ignorance and superstition than from their natural inclination, for they are seemingly as much averred to such acts of barbarity as any people in the world. We left here with the King the remainder of our cattle, viz: a Bull, two Cows and two Calves, a mail and femail, and three or 4 sheep; likewise a peacock and hen, with 3 or 4 turkeys and geese; our rabbits tho' we took great care of them were all dead but one, which of course was useless to be left here. I made no doubt but they will all thrive well, and increase very fast, for the Natives seem to be much delighted with them, and will not in the least disturb them, and will suffer them to wander about wherever they choose. The latter part of the time we lay here, we began to find fruit to grow very scarce, from our having drained this part of the Island of such as were at present ripe and fit for use; for the Natives don't care to have more than is sufficient for themselves; hogs and fowls, still remain plentifull, tho' we should naturally imagine them to grow scarce first.

After a stay of 5 or 6 weeks, we sailed from hence for the Island of Eimeo, which lies about 8 Leagues distant from this Bay; the next day we found an excellent Harbour on the north side of the Island called by the Natives Talough:[1] stood through a passage between two reefs of coral rocks laying directly opposite the entrance of the Harbour, in which we came too; it is about ⅓ of a mile wide and runs up (continuing the same width) about a mile and a half; wharped up about a mile, and the shores being bold to on each side, we hauled the ship close to; and secured Her with hawsers to the trees, being within 10 fathom of the beach. This Island is in general high; not so well cultivated as the others; which is owing in some measure to the decents and ravages sometimes made here by the Otaheiteans, who are at perpetual war with the people of this Island; who are

October 1777

Moorea, Society Islands

1 The bay was then called Tareu; now Papetoai.

not very numerous and are divided into two distinct parties,
each governed by its respective chief, but always unite in the
defence of the Country. At the head of this Harbour is a very
fertile and a delightfull valley, with a large rivulet of excellent
water running thro' it. It is entirely surrounded with hills; and
high steep cliffs affording us a great variety of the most pleasing
and romantic prospects I ever beheld. We found provision of
all kinds very scarce being barely able to procure enough for
present use, had a party on shore cutting firewood whilst we
stayed here. The Natives having stolen a small goat from us
and not returning it on Capt Cooks demanding it back, the next
morning he set out with the Marines of both ships and some
Gentlemen, in all about 35 people well armed; and marched
across part of the Island in search of it; likewise three boats
were sent manned and armed round to meet him during this
excursion. Where ever Capt Cook met with any Houses or
Canoes, that belonged to the party (which he was informed)
that had stolen the goat, he ordered them to be burnt and
seemed to be very rigid in the performance of His orders, which
every one executed with the greatest reluctance except Omai,
who was very officious in this business and wanted to fire upon
the Natives; but as they every way fled and left their all to the
mercy of the distroyers none of them were killed or hurt.
Which in all probability they would have been, had they made
the least resistance; several women and old men, still remained
by the houses whose lamentations were very great, but all their
tears and entreaties could not move Capt Cook to desist in the
smallest degree from those cruel ravages; which he continued
till the evening, when he joined the Boats, and returned
onboard having burnt and destroyed about 12 houses and as
many canoes, part of the planks he brought away with him. The
next morning he went round again with three boats where he
completed the devastation he had left undone the day before;
and all about such a trifle as a small goat which was that
evening brought onboard by the Natives. I can't well account

for Capt Cooks proceedings on this occasion as they were so very different from his conduct in like cases in his former voyages: If anything may be offered in favour of them 'twas his great friendship for Otoo (King of Otaheite) to whom these people were professed enemies.

After a stay here of about 8 days we sailed for the Island of Huaheine which lies 14 Leagues to the westward and the next day came to an anchor in Owharre [Fare] harbour, on the lee side of it; the entrance of it is between two reefs, and very narrow. Were obliged to warp up to the head of the harbour where we came to, and steadied the ship with a hawser from the shore: Omai sailed here with us in his canoe which was very large one and given him by the Admiral[1] of Otaheite. This Island is somewhat larger than Eimeo and is of a modrate hight inland. The shores in general are low and covered with trees and appears very fertile and delightfull. The Natives came onboard and supplied us with provisions in the most friendly manner imaginable, we found cocoa nuts and bread fruit in greater plenty here; and the latter much better and larger than any place we were at during the voyage; got our observatories onshore as usual. Omai, tho generally understood to have been brought from Otaheite, was in reality a native of this Island; and now chose to make it the place of his Residence in preference to any other Island in the Cluster; accordingly all our carpenters were set to work to build him a house of the planks of the canoes destroyed at Eimeo; which in about a fortnight they compleated it. His principal furniture were a bed in the English fashion, several tin pots, and kettles, and a hand organ, on which he used to play and devirt the Natives; he had likewise a brace of pistols and a musket, for which we left him a small keg of gunpowder; we also left him a horse, and a mare, for which he had a saddle and bridle and understood the management of them very well. Capt Cook purchased a small

Huahine, Society Islands

1 This was the title the ships' company bestowed upon the chief Teta'ofa (Towha). Omai bought this canoe from him for some red feathers collected in Tonga.

space of Land round his house for him from the chief, and planned out a garden in which he sowed several kinds of seeds that we brought out with us and planted some vines, brought from the cape of good Hope which seemed to prosper very well till they were plucked up in the night by some of the Natives, for which one of them was the next day brought onboard, had his ears cut off, and kept in Irons on the Quarterdeck; after he had been in confinement a week some of our people took pitty on him and released him in the night so that he made his escape; Capt Cook was exceedingly angrey on this occasion, but could by no means find out the person that did it. The Two Boys that we brought with us from New Zealand, were left here as servants to Omai; tis almost impossible to conceive their distress at being forced to part from us; it being entirely against their inclination to stay here, as it was their ernest desire to go with us to England, but that Capt Cook would not permit; they had now become so well reconciled to us, as not to have the least desire to return to their own Country. The oldest whom I mentioned before to be the Son of a chief behaved in a manner that gained him the love and esteem of every one; in all his actions he displayed a nobleness of spirit above the common rank of people; and never associated with the sailors but always kept with the Gentlemen. He was very sensible and of a mild humane dispossion and had acquired a just abhorrence of the barbarous practices of his Countrymen. The youngest was always full of mirth and good humour and for his mimicry and other little sportive tricks, was the delight of the whole ships company. So great was his desire to remain with us that he was obliged to be tied down in the canoe that carried him on shore, having leaped out of it once and attempted to swim back to the ship; the other bore it with a becoming fortitude, disdaining to ask Capt Cook for what he knew he would not grant; they were exceedingly fond of each other and every body was sorry to part with them. Omai took his leave of us in a very affectionate manner, and I believe would have been very pleased to come back to England but he knew Capt Cook would not permit him; for the curiosity of the people of England having quite subsided they began to think him rather a burthen on the publick; and were glad thus, to get clear of him. He was certainly as stupid a fellow as any on the Island and originally of the very lowest Degree; therefore I make no doubt but that he will in a short time be plundered of every-thing he has and be forced to return to his former state; but I have not the least idea of their offereing him any kind of violence. It may be wondered why the Cattle left with the King of Otaheite were not in preference given to Omai; but the reason is very obvious for as we expect every thing to be taken from him the cattle would but induce the Natives to do it sooner, and most probably would be the cause of great contentions among the Chiefs, before they could agree who were to have them and perhaps they would be destroyed to put an end to the disputes; as was done in a similar case that we met with afterwards. But should they not be hurt yet! tis most likely that they would be devided among the chiefs and ever afterward kept seperated, which would eaqually destroy the grand object of forming a breed at these Islands; but now they are perfectly free from those dangers as being in posession of the principal person of this Country. As for the Horse and Mare left with Omai, they are not of that consequence as the cattle, therefore tis no great matter what becomes of them.

Just before we sailed Capt Cook particularly desired Omai that after we had been gone about three weeks to send a canoe to us, to the Island we were going to; and if the Natives treated him ill, to send a black bead, if modrate a blew one; and if well a white one, which advice he carefully observed. After about a months stay here we sailed for Ulietea [Raiatea] which lies 8 or 9 Leagues to the westward; and the next morning came to an anchor in Ohamaneno [Haamanino] Harbour on the leeside of the Island. The entrance is between two Reefs and very narrow, wharped up about two mile; into a cove at the head of the Harbour hauled the ships close to the shore, and secured them

November 1777

Raiatea, Society Islands

with hawsers to the trees not being above 10 or 12 fathom from the beach. This Island is of a moderate height and very fertile, it is larger than Huaheine, tho' small in comparison with Otaheite, and is partly joined by a reef of shoal water upon it to an Island about 4 miles distance called Otahari; the Natives here are numorous, and supplied us with provisions in a very plentifull and friendly manner. Sent our Observatories onshore as usual; a few days after we had been in, one of our Marines who was placed as a sentinal over the observatories, was found in the night to have quited his post; and gone with his musket into the Country. In the morning the Sergeant and four Marines were sent in search of him; but returned in the evening without getting any intelligence of him. The next morning Capt Cook went in quest of him with two Boats armed and in the afternoon found him amongst a great number of the Natives, a few miles from the Harbour. He was brought onboard and punished with two dozen lashes. A little time after this a midshipman and a common sailor run away from the Discovery in the night; in the morning when Capt Cook was informed of it, he went with some boats armed in search of them and had recourse to his usual practice on these occasions; viz: of inviting some of the Chiefs onboard, and then confineing them till the Natives had made full restitution for what ever they had been guilty off; which was always found to have the disired effect, and was certainly the best method that could possibly be taken in these cases, to avoid bloodshed; being in general very easily accomplished, as the chiefs usually come onboard of their own accord two or three times a day for their amusement. In the present case Capt Clerke was ordered to get the son of Ohau, the King of the Island,[1] likewise his daughter and her husband onboard the Discovery, and confine them there, which was accoardingly done, and the King was told that they should never be released till our two deserters were brought back. He seemed to be greatly distressed on the occasion and immedi-

1 Orio, the Raiatean chief.

ately set about making enquiries after them. Capt Cook returned in the evening without getting any intilligence of them; the next morning he set out again but likewise returned without success, therefore he went no more in quest of them but depended upon the King bringing them back. During the confinement of the princes, a great number of women came round the ship and presented a very affecting scene of lamentation by tearing their hair and striking their heads with a sharks tooth that they had in each hand for that purpose, till the blood ran in a continual stream from every part of it. In this manner those Indians expressed their greif, when any great misfortunes befall them; and in the present case their appeared to be an emutation amongst them, who should carry it on to the greatest height; till the scene became too moveing to behold. One afternoon a girl that had followed us from Eimeo informed us that the Natives were then going to seize Capt Clerke and Lieut Gore, who were onshore together, by way of retalliation for the confinement of their Chiefs. Immediately the alarm was given; we were all under arms in an instant, some were sent onshore in quest of Capt Clerke, while others went in the boats along shore to seize all canoes and to fire upon the Natives where ever they saw any, to prevent them assembling together. The people that went in search of Capt Clerke and Mr Gore, found them together before the Natives had time to form an attempt; which they certainly intended, for three or four of them that were with Capt Clerke all the time he was onshore strove very much to preswade him and Mr Gore, to go into a pool of water they were standing by to bath (where all of us frequently went for that purpose); which they intended to do, but seeing the Natives so very anxious about it they began to have some suspission and declined it: upon this they began to be rather troublesome, till Capt Clerke presented a pistol at them, that he luckly chanced to have with him, which keep them quiet. Our people coming up armed a little afterwards prevented any mischief; and they returned onboard safe just before the alarm.

Capt Cook, who was onshore close to the ships was likewise perswaded to go and Bath at the same place which is nearly a mile distance but fortunately chanced to refuse, which I think plainly proves that the Natives intended to assemble there and to seize them as they were bathing, and carry them off: which by the timely intiligence we received was prevented without any bloodshed.

Our two Deserters were brought back after they had been away about a week; they had gone over in a canoe to Bolabola [Borabora], and from thence to a small Island called Tubia [Motu Iti] 12 Leagues distance from hence, where the Natives surprized them when they were asleep; and brought them onboard. They were kept in confinement during our stay at these Islands; it was well for the Natives that they delivered them up so soon for Capt Cook would very shortly have proceeded to the greatest extremities in his power to get them back, being fully determined not to suffer any person to remain here. Indeed had he once made a president of it, so very flatering was every hope of the great pleasure and happiness to be enjoyed at these Islands, together with the many hardships we had to encounter after we left them, that a great part of our people would certainly have deserted us, which would effectually have put a stop to our future proceedings. The Natives have always been extremely anxious for some of us to stay with them; and would certainly have detained the deserters and treated them with great Friendship and hospitallity had they not been obliged to deliver them up, to release their own Chiefs; they bore their confinement (which was that of not being allowed to go out of the Capt Cabin) with great fortitude and chearfulness, and seemingly without the least apprehensions of fear for their situation which was rendered as agreeable to them as circumstances could possibly admit of.

About three of four weeks after we had been here, a canoe arrived from Omai, which brought a white bead; which shows that he was still treated in a friendly manner. Tis somewhat surprizing that the Indian who had his ears cut off at Huaheine for plucking the vines up in Omai's gardens, and was kept in confinement onboard for some time till he was suffered to make his escape, should have the confidence to appear here in public along side the ships and seemingly without the least fear of being brought onboard to his former confinement. Capt Cook who certainly must have seen him, took not the least notice of him.

We had compleated our wood and water and had now salted about 12 puncheons of pork for sea, since we came amongst these Islands; we likewise took a great quantity of green plantains from this place to carry to sea as a substitute for bread.

Our stay here was about a month from whence we sailed for Bolobolo. The interior part of this Island is a high peeked mountain; the shores are low and covered with trees, having a very fertile and delightfull appearance; we lay too off an excellent Harbour,[1] on the SW side of the Island, where Capt Cook with 3 or 4 Boats well armed went on shore to purchase a small kedge anchor that had been left by the French[2] at Oaitepeha [Vaitapiha] Bay, and was brought by the Natives to the King of this Island as a present; we purchased it of him for a few hatchets. The fluke and ring was broke off, so that it was of no other use but to work up into traid for the Indians. This Island tho small was very powerfull, and excepting Otaheite, Eimeo, Oznaburg [Mehetia] (which lay some distant to windward) had by some means made the others tributary to it. We did not stop here but after a stay of four months at these Islands we sailed from them on the 10th of December 1777 for the NW Coast of America, there to prosecute our grand object: the Search of a NW passage to India.

These Islands are 9 in number and situated between 17° 55' and 16° 25' South Latitude and 207° 40' East Longitude. Otaheite which is by far the largest is in the form of two circles

Margin notes:
December 1777

Borabora, Society Islands

The Society Islands

1 Teavanui.
2 Bougainville in 1768.

joined by an Isthmus of low land; one of them is six and half the other three and half Leagues Diameter. Ulietea[1] which is the next largest, is about the size of little Otaheite; Eimeo, Huaheine, Otaha and Bolobolo are nearly alike and are each about 7 miles in extent. Morua and Oznaburg, are two small high Islands, and Tubai is three small low patches of land joined by a Coral Reef of rocks. They are very fertile, and populous being supposed altogether to contain 100,000 Inhabitants; their productions are cocoa nuts, bread fruit, plantains Bananoes, eddyroot, a few sugar canes, and a particular kind of Fruit found only in these Seas: its about the size of an orange, it is covered with a smooth Rind like that of a plumb of a bright yellow and has a large prickley core; it is of a different flavour to any other fruit and is very delicious; they have likewise a small kind of apple which is very insipid. The only yams we met with at these Islands were a few small ones of a particular kind at Eimeo. Tis very surprizing that several of the fruits of the East and West Indies such as oranges, limes, pine apples, mellons, citrons, tamarinds, figs, are not found at any of the Islands we visited in the South Seas – tho they lie in the same Climate; yet any of them transplanted there might be brought to great perfection; as the fruit they have are superior to those of the same kind in any other Country.

On Capt Cooks arrival at Matavai Bay in his second voyage he enclosed a small spot of ground for a garden wherein he sowed the seeds of several kinds of European vegetables, which sprung up very rapidly and seemed to thrive exceeding well: but when we went to look at them this voyage we found them entirely destroyed, and the places over grown with weeds; yet I make no doubt but with a few Europeans to attend them, that every kind of fruit and vegetable that can possibly be produced in an hot Climate would come to great perfection, in the fertile

1 The islands he describes, in order of reference, are: Raiatea, Tahiti Iti (the eastern end of Tahiti), Moorea, Huahine, Tahaa, Borabora, Maupiti, Mehetia, and Motu Iti.

soil of these Islands. Their only Quadrupeds are Hogs, dogs and rats. Fowls are very plentifull; they have very few birds, and those small and no way remarkable. The Natives of these Islands are tall strong and well formed, their complexion is of a very light copper colour and fairer than any other we met with during the voyage; they have a very pleasing countenance which more resemble that of an European than an Indian; they are of a mild generous and agreeable dispossion, but are very indolent and rather effeminate, not having that manly and warlike appearance that we find in the people of the Friendly Islands. The women are the most beautifull we have met with in the South Seas: they are of the most mild and pleasing dispossion imaginable, are always full of gaiety and good humour, and in fact are possessed of every qualification that can render them agreeable. They are exceeding neat in their persons, and also in their dress; which consists only of two pieces of cloth one wraped round their waists reaching below their knees and the other thrown carelessly over their shoulders which is very cool and agreeable in those climates; some of them at times when the weather is sultry, wear a kind of bonnet made of green flap to shade their faces from the rays of the sun. Tho' the manners of those Ladies, are not polished or refined by education, nor their dress aided by ornaments, yet! in their native innocence and simplicity they are more elegant and engageing, than can well be conceived. Their songs and dances, which are very frequent, appear exceeding lascivious in the eyes of an European; but in them every Idea of the kind is removed, by the custom of the Country: which seemingly permits them to pursue the natural impulse of their passions. Here, likewise they are not permitted to eat in the presence of the men. Most of the Indians that we have seen in the South Seas have a custom of what they call tattowing; that is marking themselves in various parts of their bodies by introducing a black oily liquid under the skin, by perforation. The instrument they use for this purpose is a thin flat peice of bone; the lower

edge is of different sizes, from an inch to a ¼ of an inch in
breadth, and full of sharp pointed teeth very close together;
which they dip in the liquid, and holding it very slitely by the
handle, apply it to the parts to be marked, and with a small stick
in the other hand they strike litely upon the head of it till the
teeth pierce the skin sufficient to admit the liquid thro the
punctures; very little blood is drawn in this operation which is
less painfull than would be imagined. In 5 or 6 days the parts
are perfectly healed and leaves a dark blue stain that cannot be
obliterated. The natives here, and at the Friendly Islands, are
tattooed with broad lines round their hips and thighs, and
various small figures of men, dogs, birds all very badly
executed upon their arms and legs, but have no marks upon
their faces like the New Zealand Chiefs; who are tattooed there
very curiously in Spiral lines, which greatly adds to the natural
ferocity of their countenances. Several of our people got marks
of various kinds done by the Natives. The difference between
houses here and at the Friendly Islands is that these are
considerably larger, the lower part of the roof higher (being
from 6 to 9 feet from the ground) and that the greatest part of
them instead of having the sides quite open, have them
inclosed with peices of bamboo set upright in the ground at the
distance of 3 or 4 inches from one another; which reach up to
the roof except a space of 6 or 8 feet that is left to enter in at,
across which they have a fence about two feet high to keep the
hogs and fowls out which are exceedingly tame, and domestic.
This kind of inclosure affords no shelter from the weather but,
however, this delightfull climate requires no other but that of
the roof to keep the rain and rays of the Sun from them. Besides
their dwelling houses which are very much scattered they have
here and there particular ones for their public meetings, and
devertions, which are very large and commodious being from
140 to 180 feet in length and 30 and 40 feet in breadth, and are
without any partitions; the sailing canoes here are sometimes
two joined parallel to each other by planks lashed athwart both

of them; and sometimes a single one with a small platform across it, and an out rigger to prevent it upseting; they have only one mast which stands upright in the middle of them and one yard and a sail made of mats sewed together which is very narrow. They are much smaller than those for war and sails but indifferently; their single canoes have outriggers like those of the friendly Islands, but are clumsey and very ill built. The principal part of their cultivations at these Islands is that of the cloth tree[1] which they plant in low ground; and about two feet asunder; and as they spring up pluck off the young buds that shoot out from the sides of them reserving only those at the top; by this means they grow very fast and when they come to be about 6 feet high are cut down before the bark begins to harden, which is the only part they make use of. The process of making it into Cloth is as follows: after the green outside is stripped off, they take the inner part and put it in water to soak for a few days till it become soft like pork; they then take it out and spread it close upon a flat board and beat it together while it is wet with a square piece of hard wood about a foot and half in length and each side 2½ inches in breadth which are all fluted; the first side they make use of has about fives grooves in an inch, and the other three are finer in such proportion that the last side they beat with, has about 18; this part of the operation they continue till it is of a proper thickness and is sufficiently connected, being when wet of a very cohesive quality; after that they let it remain upon the board till it is dry, which ends the process. Its natural colour is white which in general they let remain so. Some few pieces are painted red; it is about twice the strength of paper of the same thickness, and will not bear to be handled when wet unless very tenderly. Some pieces they make as thick as our broad cloth which is done by putting two or three thin ones upon one another when they are wet and not above half beat and then pressing them together; these generally have one side painted

1 The *aute*, or paper mulberry, from which the Tahitian bark-cloth, *tapa*, was made.

yellow which is some times ornamented with small red circles and spots; the only colours they have got are black, yellow and red. The Chiefs often wear a piece of this kind loose over their shoulders, which reaches down to their waists, having a hole cut thro the middle of it, thro which they put their heads. The Cloth is much better here and they make far greater quantities of it than at the Friendly Islands, where the process is the same, but there they have none of the thick kind. The thin pieces which are the largest are made into Bales of various sizes, being from 15 to 40 yards in length and from two to six in breadth; this manufactory is principally performed by the women. There is a particular kind of root here called by the Natives Yaa-va[1] which is very scarce and used only by the Chiefs after it is prepared in the following manner. Four or five of their attendants sit down by a large wooden bowl, and take each of them a mouthfull of this root, and chew it for three or four minutes, till it is sufficiently tore to pieces and made soft; they then take it out and put it into the Bowl and take another mouthfull, which they chew in the same manner till they have got a sufficient quantity; to this they pour some water, and stir it round with their hands; and squeeze it till all the juice is out of the root, which makes the water thick and of a light yellow. They then strain it thro' a piece of cloth and the Chiefs drink it immediately; afterwards seemingly with as much pleasure as an European does the richest wines, till they become quite intoxicated with it. The people of the Friendly Islands make use of it in the same manner.

The fish at these Islands are small and not very plentifull, the few they get are caught either with a very fine seine or with a hook and line. They are remarkably fond of them, and eat them either raw or broiled according to the taste of individuals. Their fishing lines and seines are made of the fibers of the bark of the

---

1 *Yava,* or *kava,* is a mildly narcotic infusion prepared from the roots of a pepper plant. It was drunk more commonly in the Western Pacific (Samoa, Fiji) but not at all in New Zealand.

cloth tree; and their hook of mother of pearl, which is very plentifull here – these are exceeding neat and curious and superior to any we have seen. Their method of producing fire, here and at all the Islands in the South Seas, is by the friction of two pieces of soft dry wood rubbed violently together for some time which has the desired effect. They are exceeding dexterous at theiving, and seldome let slip an opportunity when ever it affords; which obliged us to be always upon our guard, to privent it. The articles of traid with which we purchased provisions: were hatchets, nails, knives, white beads, and red feathers, especially the latter, which they esteem of greater value than any thing else we could offer them; their own hatchets are stone, there being no iron or any other kind of metal in these Islands. This seems to be the principal mechanical Tool they are possesed of, having no other to fell their trees with which are of a hard kind of wood, and to cut out the plank where with they make their Canoes; which renders these proformances very tedious and laborious and it is surprizing how they accomplish so many under such circumstances. They are very assidious in procuring our hatchets or iron in any form being well convinced of its use. The language spoke here varies very little from that of New Zealand and the Friendly Islands. Their religion tho' it is attended with some superstitious practices; yet! the principals of it, are as natural, and agreeable to reason, as what is taught in most of the churches in Europe; they pay their adorations to a supreme Being, whom they believe to be Omnipotent – Omniscient and far beyond their comprehention; and they hope after this life, to enjoy a more exalted and happy state in his immediate presence.

The most regular form of Government at these Islands, is that of great Otaheite, which some what resembles the German. The Country is devided into several Districts which are Subject to their respective Cheifs of whom the King is the head, who from the small respect paid him by the Natives seem to be invested with no great degree of Authority, having but little power of his own without the joint consent and assistance of the Chiefs, who don't appear to be in the least inclined to acts of despotism any further than is necessary to enforce the laws of the Country: by which those that have property are perfectly secure in it, and the lower class who have not got any are dependent on them that have, without the most distant signs of Slavery and opposition. The other Islands in this Cluster are governed nearly in the same manner. These Islanders beyond a doubt live in the most perfect state of freedom, friendship, and happiness, of any people in the world: and still enjoy all the pleasures of the Golden Age which is now nowhere else to be found. The mode of Government at the Friendly Islands seem to be somewhat different to that here; for the principal Cheifs there appear to have much greater Authority over the Natives, and were rather inclined to be arbitrary.

We left these Islands with the greatest regret immaginable; as supposing all the pleasures of the voyage to be now at an end; having nothing to expect in future but excess of cold, hunger, and every kind of hardship and distress attending a Sea life in general, and these voyages in particular; the idea of which rendered us quite dejected.

From the Society Islands we directed our course to the Northward, having a moderate breeze and pleasant weather; on the 25th of December we discovered a low sandy Island, with a large Lagoon in the middle of it into which there was an opening on the leeside off which we came to an anchor in betwixt 12 and 20 fathom of water, and good ground about a Christmas mile from the shore; this Island which we called Christmas lies Island in Lat: 2° North and Long: 202° East; it is 6 Leagues in extent and is an entire Sandbank, almost level with the water, having the most dreary appearance that can possibly be conceived; there are two small copses of cocoanut trees upon it and a few bushes scattered here and there with scarce any verdure on them; we found no inhabitants upon it, it being impossible for any human being to exist here on this barren spot, which is frequented only by sea birds of various kinds that resort here in great numbers to lay their eggs; which we found very plentifull upon the sand but scarce one in twenty without a young one in it. The Shores being very rockey and a great surf breaking on them rendered the landing every way very difficult; except within the Lagoon, into which there is a good passage for boats. Sent parties onshore in different places to catch Turtle, which are exceeding plentifull here; the method is, to watch them in the night when they come upon the beach to sleep, and then approaching to them by surprize, turn them upon their backs before they get into the water; after which they can't stir from the spot. The people onshore suffered great distress for want of water there being none fresh upon the Island, and we could scarce send it from the ship fast enough; several of them were forced to drink the turtle blood to quench their thirst. The heat was so intense as to raise such blisters upon their faces, the lips in particular, that some of them was obliged to be brought onboard. One of the people belonging to the Discovery was missing three days, after which he was found almost famished and so weak that he could scarce stand having had nothing to drink all the time but the blood of birds and turtles which he had killed; he had gone out of sight of the boat and could not find his way back, there being no rising ground for him to get upon to look for the ships. Caught plenty of excellent large fish here, with hook and line. The plantains that we brought with us from Ulietea [Raiatea] and were served to us in lieu for bread being now finished we were put to ⅔ allowance of biscuit. This was the first time of our using any spiecies of ships provisions except a small quantity of spirits since the Day that we anchored at the Friendly Islands which was a space of 8 months. This great supply not only refreshed and strengthened us as much as if we had just left England, but enabled us to prosacute our Discoveries to the Northwards a second season and was in great mesure a compensation for that we lost in not being able to fetch Otaheite the first time. During our stay here, which was about a week we caught upwards of

200 turtle which we carried to sea with us; they were of the green kind, and in general very large.

From hence we continued our course to the Northwards being a modrate traid wind and fine weather; about the 25th of January 1778 being then in Lat: 21° North Long: 201° East we discovered an Island [Oahu] at the distance of 10 Leagues to windward of us and in a few hours afterwards another to
leeward which we stood for; and the next day came to an anchorage in an open road on the South side of it having bad ground and a Reef to leeward of us. This Island was called by
the Natives Towi [Kauai]: it is of a circular form and about the size of Otaheite; the interior parts are high and the shore in general is of a modrate height and has a very barren appearance till you come close in with it; what verdure there is being only in the vallies, which are very fertile. The Natives came off to us in their Canoes in great numbers as soon as we came near the shore; and were very easily perswaded to come onboard, which they ventured to do without the least diffidence; they appeared to be much delighted and took a fancy to several things that they saw, and were going very leisurely without any scruple of hesitation to carry them into their canoes; and seemed greatly surprized at our preventing it by taking from them what they had got hold of, which they would not quit till after some persuasion; for they could not believe that we were in earnest but imagined that we would allow them to take what they chose till we convinced them to the contrary, and then they were perfectly satisfied, and behaved in a very agreeable and friendly manner. In their persons and dress they very much resembled the Friendly Islanders and spoke nearly the same language as the Otaheitains. When they had fully satisfied their curiosity, and were returning to the shore, as soon as they had got a little distance from the ships, we preceived them heaving a great number of small stones out of the bottom of their canoes into the water; whether they brought them off to act with on the defensive or offencive we could not possitively determine but

from every appearence were rather led to believe the former. A boat was sent on shore from each ship with a view to purchase provisions; when immediately they came near the beach the Natives surrounded them in great numbers, upon which they did not think it prudent to land but remained in the Boats. The Natives soon began to be very troublesome and even attempted to haul the boat onshore which obliged the Officers to fire at them by which one of them was killed. The report of the musket together with the fire and smoak, and the execution it did, being what they had never seen before and a mystry, they could form not the least conception of, terrified them so much, that they all quited the boats instantly and went away carring the dead body off with them and making great lamantations; the boats did not attempt to land after this, but returned onboard. The next morning Capt Cook went onshore himself with 4 or 5 boats well armed to purchas provisions and bring off water. He had no sooner landed but a number of the Natives came and prostrated themselves before him in the most submissive manner imaginable. The reason of this he was unacquainted with as he had not been informed that one of them had been killed the day before; they brought plenty of provisions down to the beach consisting of hogs, fowls, bread fruits, plantains, eddy root, sweet potatoes and sugar cane, in great quantities, which we purchased with hatchets, nails, beads; our red feathers, being no article of traid here, they having got plenty of them. Tis rather surprizing that there are no cocoa nuts here, which are found in all the other Islands. The Natives came off to the ships again, and brought with them the productions of the Island which we purchased alongside. There is a large rivulet of excellent water here but the great surf that runs upon the beach renders the watering rather difficult; however each ship got off three or four boat loads. After we had been here three or four days the wind came on to blow fresh along shore, which caused a great swell that the boats could not land; and Capt Cook not thinking it safe riding in the situation we were in, we hove up and stood out to Sea with an intention to look for a safer anchorage, leaving the Discovery still in the road. We had no sooner got a little distance from the land but the wind shifted directly off the shore which entirely frustrated our design, for tho' we attempted to work up for four or five days, we could not get to windward; therefore giving over all hopes of fetching into anchorage again, we stood for an Island that lies in sight to the West, at about 8 leagues distance and the next morning came to an anchor in an open road on the lee side of it. This Island is

Niihau   called by the Natives Neehow [Niihau]; it is about ⅓ of the extent of that we left and has the most Barren appearence imaginable not having a Tree upon it. The weathermost part of it is of a modrate height but the leeside off which we lay, is low and swampy; the landing is attended with great difficulty from the surf that breaks upon the shore, which is very rockey. The water here is in standing pools, and is but indifferent and very troublesome to get at. There appeared to be but few inhabitants upon this Island, who came off to us and behaved very friendly. Hogs and Fowls, are exceeding scarce here; there are plenty of yams, and sweet potatoes, which seemed to be the only produce of the Island. For we saw no fruit upon it; the Discovery came in the next day from Towi and informed us that they had purchased a great quantity of yams while we were out; we did not see any when we were there, the Natives not having brought them down there. Sent a party onshore with a tent to purchase yams; and as bread was the scarcest article of provision we had onboard they became a great object to us as being an excellent substitute for it, and will good two or three months at sea, plantains or Bananoes if brought away green will keep two or three weeks, but are indifferent substitute. Sweet potatoes which are excellant eating will not keep above 10 days but the bread fruit will remain good only two or three days.

February   After we had been here about a week the wind began to blow
1778   fresh off shore; it came on in the night which draged our anchor into deep water; we immediately hove it up and made sail and

stood out to Sea, having luckily got our tent and people from the shore the day before. We saw a small high Island laying about 8 or 10 Leagues to the westward which we were told by the people of Neehow is uninhabited: having a light breeze, we did not loose sight of the land for two days, which was on the 12th of February 1778. To these Islands Capt Cook gave the name of Sandwich;[1] which I shall defer giving any further descriptions of till we come to them again.

1 After the Earl of Sandwich, first Lord of the Admiralty.

Chapter Three

SEARCH FOR A NORTH-WEST PASSAGE

We continued our course to the Northward, and to the Eastward, as much as the wind would admit having modrate weather. The yams that we brought with us were served at the rate of a pound per man; and lasted about a fortnight but the Discovery had them much longer, after that we were put to ⅔ allowance of bread and had the pork served that we had salted at the Society Islands, which lasted out the greatest part of the season and kept very good all the time. We were allowed a small quantity of sowr Krout, twice a week to eat with our salt provisions; it is an excellent antiscorbutick and keept exceeding well all the voyage. We had likewise portable soup, three times a week boiled with our peas; which were much the worst article of provisions we had onboard; for they had been kiln dried to keep them which almost rendered them useless: for after being in the copper for six hours they were very little softer than at first, and only just tinged the water they were boiled in. We found the cold to encrese very fast, as we advanced to the northwards; and hunger accompanying it, for our allowance of bread was very short and we had no flower seved in lieu of Beef, which was grown very bad.

On the 7th of March 1778 we made the westward Coast of North America in Lat: 45° and Long: 235½° East; which is

March
1778

about 8 Degrees to the East of what was layed down in the best
Charts – we found it to trend North and South without the least
signs of a bay or inlet; the inland parts are very mountanious
but the shore is of a modrate height. The appearance of this
Country was very different to which we had been use to
between the tropicks, it being entirely covered with snow which
afforded a very dreary prospect; there being not the least
verdure to be seen. We were forced by contrary winds to stand
along shore to the southward as far as Cape Blanc, which lies in
Lat: 43° North; and is the Norther most Land that was seen by
Sir Francis Drake in his Discoveries of New Albion. The wind
now became favourable, we hauled off the land and stood to the
Northward and fell in with it again where we first made it; the
weather being modrate we stood within two miles of the shore
which was thinly covered with wood and terminated in several
long sandy beaches; we sounded off here and had 40 fathoms of
water. From hence we treaced the coast in a northerly direction
up to the Lat: 49½° North, where we first saw the appearance
of an Inlet. The wind being favourable we stood directly for it,

Nootka
Sound

and got in that evening; which was on the 20th of March[1], a
fortnight from our first reaching the Land. To this Inlet which
lies in the above Lat: and Longitude 234° East, Capt Cook
gave it the name of King George Sound. The mouth of it is
about 5 miles across but it does not continue that breadth above
3 miles before it separates into two channels, each about a mile
wide which are formed by what appeared to be a large Island
Laying in the middle of the sound: with several small ones
laying off that end of it, towards the entrance; we stood about a
mile up the Eastermost Channel where we anchored for the
night in 85 fathom of water two cables from the nearest shore.
As soon as we came near the Land several of the Natives came
off in their Canoes within about ½ a mile of the ships but could

1 Gilbert's dates are here in error. It was March 31 before the ships found anchor
   in what is now called Nootka Sound, on the West coast of Vancouver Island,
   where they were to remain for four weeks.

not be perswaded to come alongside; they followed us up the channel; and continued paddling round us after we came to anchor till late, singing all the time very loud in a manner not at all disagreeable; they visited us again in the morning, and ventured to come onboard, and behaved very friendly. The only thing they brought with them were dryed skins and a few small dryed fish that were scarce eatable, which we purchased with the usual articles. We warped the ships up to a small cove near us upon the Island where we hauld close in and stedied with hawsers to the trees. We set up our Observatories upon a Rock which lay within about a cable length of us, and was very convenient, for that purpose; and immediately began unrigging the ship, for geting the Foremast out having discovered a spring in the head of it a little before we came in; we got it on shore upon a small stoney beach near us and had new cheeks put on it which we cut in the woods. During the time the Foremast was repairing we had some very hard squalls off the Land and having our mizen topmast up and topsail yard accross, the wind took such hold of them as to cause something to crack about the top. We instantly struck the yard and topmast and on unrigging the mizen mast found an old spring in the weak of the rigging, right a throa'rt the head of the mast which had been greatly enlarged by the above mentioned squalls. We then set about getting it out and in lowering it over the side; the head chancing to take the quarter gallry proved so rotten as to break short off where the spring was – therefore it was very luckey that we found it out before we went to sea again.

We were visited every day by a party of the Natives who came early in the morning and returned in the evening to their village; which lay at some distance from us. We had this kind of intercourse with them for about a fortnight quite undesturbed, till one morning we perceived a number of Canoes full of people well armed coming into the cove a different way from what those did that were with us; who as soon as they saw them likewise began to arm themselves and retired to the beach close

April
1778

astern of the ship, from which we naturally supposed they
intended jointly to attack us; therefore got ready to receive
them and sent some men armed upon the rock to protect the
Observatories – in this expectation for two or three hours, the
strange party laying all that time in their Canoes near the ship,
and the others on shore, both with their weapons in their hands;
and talking very much amongst themselves. Capt Cook not
being thoroughly sensitive from their manners what their
intentions were, was unwilling to fire at them, till they began to
attack, tho' he was once very near it as they approached close
alongside of us; at last we discovered it to be a quarral betwixt
the two parties, and that the dispute was the right of trading
with us; which after several long harangues, and threatening
gestures, on both sides, was happily decided without their
proceeding to greater extremities: and both parties traided with
us ever afterwards in a very peaceable manner, and friendly.

A few days after this, two large parties of Canoes full of men
with arms, were seen off the entrance of the cove; they each
came a different way and approached to one another, within a
short distance, then stoped and lay still at about ½ a mile from
the ships; we were all in expectation that they were coming to
an action as one party stood up, shoke their weapons at the
other, and made every motion for fighting; by way of a
challenge, as we supposed, singing at the same time and beating
their paddles against their Canoes for the space of half an hour.
They then set down very quietly and the other party stood up
and acted in the same manner; this, they continued to do
alternately for four or five times, and then withdrew out of
sight. They had very often little quarrels with one another
alongside, which generally ended with pulling each others hair;
this they would do for near half an hour together, without the
least motion till one of them gave out, being apparently of a very
obstinate dispossion. When their disputes do not run so high as
to require weapons to decide them, this seems to be the only
method they make us of; having no idea of striking with their

hands, which is rather surprizing, as boxing is generally practised by most other Indians.

As soon as our foremast was repaired we got it in and then set about choseing a tree for a mizen mast; of which there were great plenty fit for the purpose but the difficulty lay in finding one that after we had felled it, we could get down to the beach, or into the water, for they stood so thick that in falling, they generally got jammed betwixt one another; after three or four attempts with great labour, we got one down to the beach which the Carpenters of both ships set to work upon.

Finding some of our main rigging much worn we set up an entire new gang; and chose the best from the old main and fore rigging to set up forewards. After we had been here about three weeks the Natives began to bring onboard some small fish to sell, that were then coming into season; which tho' very scarce yet! were a comfortable supply to us in the hungry state we were in. We found a Run of water close above the beach from which we compleated the ships and likewise with wood from the same place; we cut several small spars here for standing sail booms, yards, and a large one that we made into a topmast which tho' it then appeared to be very good, yet, during the voyage it entirely decayed as it lay upon the booms; our new mizen mast being finished we got it in, and converted the old one into an excellent main topmast. Capt Cook with two boats well armed, made an excursion up the sound and found the two channels to meet at about four Leagues distance from the entrance, forming a large Island as we had conjected. They met with four or five villages in different parts of the sound, which appeared to be inhabited by parties unconnected with each other; they landed at two or three of them and were received by the Natives in a very friendly manner. A few days before we left this place one of our Gentlemen purchased from the Natives two silver spoons, which we supposed they got from the Spaniards at California; and had handed them from one to another along the coast, as we could not learn that any ships had been here before.

Being now as compleatly refitted as our stores and the Country would admit of, after a stay of five weeks we sailed from hence on the 27th of April 1778.

This part of the Coast is very mountanious and the tops of the Hills were still covered with snow; the Shores in general are high, steep, and rockey, and covered with tall straight pines, of a very large growth. There are very few beaches here, and the underwood is so thick, that we were entirely deprived of the pleasure of walking up into the Country, being scarce able to get an hundred yards from the water. The soil appears to be fertile but is nowhere cultivated; we found gooseberries and currant trees, and strawberry plants, growing wild in the woods, and were just coming into blosom when we sailed. The quadrupeds of this Country are black Bears, Wolves, Deer, Foxes, Racoons, Martins and Beavers; we purchased several of the dried skins of these animals from the Natives, who have them in great plenty, particularly those of the Land and Sea Beavers, but of the two the latter is the most plentifull, the fur of which is supposed to be superior to any that is known. The most valuable articles that we used in this traffick were hatchets, saws, old swords, large knives, and blew beads; but having very few of any of them left, we supplied the want of them with pewter, plates, pieces of iron hoops, old buckles, buttons and in fact, anything made of iron, tin, copper or brass. The principle motive of our procuring those skins, was for clothing to secure us against the cold. For of the bearskins we made greatcoats, and with the others, lined our Jackets, and made caps and gloves, from which we found great comfort; and indeed we had need for we experienced very little from our provisions, which were only just sufficient to keep us alive.

The Natives at this place tho' much more numerous than on any other part of the coast that we touched at, yet! are few in comparison to what we met with amongst the Tropical Islands.

They are of a smaller stature than any we saw during the voyage, rarely exceeding five feet, yet are robust and well proportioned, their faces are very broad and flat; but their features are rather small, they are of a ruddy complexion and if they kept themselves clean would be modrately fair; they paint their foreheads very curiously in a veriety of forms, and colours, but chiefly in squares, which are of one colour and the broad lines they are formed of, with another. Their hair which they wear long is cloted together with a red mixture much resembling that used by the New Zealanders both in colour, and smell, but still more disagreeable to appearence. In their dispossions they are savage and obstinate; yet! seem to have but a small share of natural bravery. Their dress consists cheifly in furs and the skins of such animals as they kill in hunting, made into a kind of frock or jacket, reaching below their knees; instead of this they sometimes wear a cloak, made of long fine grass platted together like the New Zealand ones, but not half so neatly manufactured. They likewise wear a round cap, ending in a point at the top like those of the Chinese. These people both in their persons and dress are certainly the most uncleanly and filthy set we ever met with. They are very carefull of their women for I don't remember that more than two or three of them came off to the ships. They were dressed nearly in the same manner as the men and like them had the most dirty appearance immaginable; being far unlike the blooming beauties of the Tropicks. Their Language is the most unpleasing I ever heard, having a very harsh gutteral sound and there are several words in it that even themselves have great difficulty in pronouncing. The Houses here are the most ill built; and considering the Climate afford the least shelter of any we have seen. Their Canoes are broad flat bottomed, resembling a Norway yaul; and in general seem to be cut our of one tree.

The Arms used by those Indians, are bows and arrows, and long wooden spears. Their bows are the best I ever saw, and are rendered very strong and elastick by having a number of Whale

sinews along the grove in the back of them, and being closely
bound round with the same from one end to the other; their
arrows are made of fir and headed with hard wood, bone or
flint, and some few with copper roughly beat out, which seem to
be very scarce among them tho' they certainly get it in this
Country. Several of their spears are pointed in the same
manner.

The principal mode of fishing here and all along the Coast is
with small Darts, four or five feet in length, to which they have
a long small line made of sinews ready to wear out, as soon as
they have struck the fish; they are headed either with bone, or a
piece of hard wood, four or five inches long, which is mostly
barbed all the way up. In general they have but one prong; but
some of them have three. Those Darts are for small fish but for
whale they have a different kind. The head of it is a piece of
wood about four inches long with a thick line fast to the middle
of it; one end is pointed with a muscle shell ground flat, and to a
point, and fastend into the wood with the kind of gum; on the
other end is a hole into which, when they want to use it, they put
the end of a long staff for the purpose of darting it into the
Whale; the staff coming out and leaving the head behind buries
in the flesh, with a long line to it ready to wear out.

These people don't seem to have any Cheifs amongst them,
as we find in the Tropickal Islands; but live in Families quite
independent of one another. Their sustenance principally
depends on their success in fishing and hunting in which they
spend the greater part of their time; and being very dexterous in
both procure a moderate support.

They used frequently as they lay alongside in their Canoes
to entertain us with their war songs, and a very curious kind of
masquerade dance; in which they put on large wooden masks,
of various forms and colours, and shifted them with great
dexterity. The greater part of them resembled the face of a man;
the features were cut out larger but very expressive and well
executed, and represented a number of droll gestures and

distortions; they had hair, eyebrows and teeth to them and were painted very curiously; some of them were made to resemble the heads of wild beasts, and others, that of a bird with the bill to open and shut at pleasure. The two latter ones they frequently made use of in hunting, by way of deception to decoy those animals near them that they are in search off.

After leaving this place our intention was to keep along shore; but before I proceed any further it will be necessary to mention that some parts of the coast we were going to explore had been slightly sketched by Behring[1] and Tehiribrow,[2] two Russian navigators who sailed from Kamchatka upon Discoveries in these seas in the years 1728 and 1741. We had no sooner got out of the sound but the same evening a very hard gale came on directly off the land, attended with the most severe squalles we had yet experienced, which drove us quite off the coast. The ship very unfortunately too at this time sprung a leak in her starboard buttock acasioned by the violence of the gale which obliged us to stand to the North and to keep her upon that Tack. The fish and spirit rooms were intirely filled with water, which rendered our situation rather alarming, as knowing the ship was much decayed in her after parts. The people were now put to two watches and kept constantly employed at the hand pumps and bailing with buckets, yet! could scarce keep the leak under. In this disagreeable situation we remained for two days after which the gale abated; and the weather coming on modrate, we made no more water than we could keep clear with one pump.

The wind still continuing from the East we were not able to make the Land, till we got up to the Latitude of 56°N and Longitude 226½°E. So that a space of 153 Leagues unfortunately remains unexplored: from hence we treaced it in a NW to N direction up to 60°, where we was becalmed for 4 or 5 days at about 6 Leagues distance from the shore which had a

May
1778

1 Vitus Bering.
2 Alexei Chirikov.

very dreary appearance; having no wood upon it and being entirely covered with snow. There are two high mountains (covered with snow) here, laying close to the shore and about 15 Leagues distant from each other; the Northermost which is the largest is loftier than any we have seen before, and is called Mount St. Elias by the Russians, who landed near this place and had a boats crew cut of by the Natives; a breeze springing up, we stood along the coast which from hence trends to the WNW.

On the 12th of May, about noon, we discovered an opening[1] which had a very promising appearance; as the weather being hazy, we could not see any land within it. Having a favourable

Prince William Sound

wind we bore away for it immediately flattering our selves with the hope of having found the passage we were in search of. By 4 o'clock we got up to it; and found it to be about 4 Leagues wide but had scarce stood into it, before we saw two high bluff points open one after the other on the Eastside; which we had no sooner passed but we were obliged to come to an anchor about a quarter of a mile from the shore, by reason of a very thick fog coming on, which rendered it too hazardous to proceed any further at the time. A boat was sent on Shore with a few people to haul the seine for Fish, we caught several cod alongside with hook and line which were a most welcome acquisition to us being almost starved with Hunger; we had no idea from the appearance of the Country, it being entirely covered with snow, that there were any Inhabitants here, till our people that were upon the beach hauling the seine saw two large Canoes[2] full of men making towards them; upon which having no Arms, they instantly put off from the shore and returned onboard without having caught any fish. The Natives came off within about a cables length of the ships and paddled around them three or four times singing and hallowing all the time very loud but we

---

1 Prince William Sound, named Sandwich by Cook.
2 There were mixed groups, both Indian and Eskimo, making seasonal visits to the Sound.

could not entice them to come alongside; they continued to reconiter us about two hours and then returned to the shore.

The next morning the weather being tolerably clear our hope of a passage in a great measure vanished upon seeing land all round us. We now weighed and stood further up to the Northward but in the afternoon the wind coming on to blow fresh with hard rain and a thick fog we were again obliged to stop and work up into a cove on the East shore where we came too, and steadied with a small anchor and hawser. The weather cleared up in the morning, we preceived that we had got into a large sound to which Capt Cook gave the name of Sandwich but is since altered to Prince William Henry; it lies in Lat: 60½°N and Long: 213° East and is 325 Leagues to the NW of King Georges sound. The interior parts of the Country is very mountainous, the shore is in general steep and rockey and thinly covered with pines which are of a small growth. The Natives came off to us a little after daylight and ventured to come onboard the ships; they brought with them great numbers of skins which we purchased with the usual articles; that of the sea beaver we found very plentifull. A boat was sent with the Master to go round a low point about a mile from us to sound and look for water; he had no sooner come near the shore, but he preceived several Canoes in pursuit of him, which obliged him to put back and had scarce time to get clear of them. The weather being modrate we heeled the ship to port as much as possible to examine the leak on the starboard buttock before mentioned; which we were lucky enough to bring above water, it being close below the wale and occasioned by some of the seems being very open and the oakum quite rotten and great part of it got out. In two days we repaired this defect being obliged to put two and half inch rope along the seams which were too wide for caulking. During this time we compleated our water from a rivulet near us in the cove; wild Ducks and Geese seem to be very plentifull here, but are so shy that we shot very few of them. About an hour after the Natives first came off to us, three or four of them very leisurely got out of their Canoes into our cutter that was laying alongside: the others af the same time handed them Arms and were going to take her away with two or our men that were in her; till the people onboard preceived it, and drove them out, nor did they quit her till they were absolutely forced to it. A little afterward, some of them alongside the Discovery chanced to go onboard when the people were below at breakfast, and the ship being flush fore and aft therefore they saw but two or three that were upon deck, looking out; from which they supposed there were no more belonging to her and that they should be able to take possession of her.

Accordingly they dispatched a Canoe to acquaint those that were with us, who all instantly paddled away to the Discovery to assist them, thinking to have a valuable prize. Several of them now ventured onboard and laid hold of such moveable things as came first to hand, and were going very deliberately to carry them into their Canoes till they were prevented by the people coming on Deck with cutlasses at which they seemed much surprized, and quited what they had hold of very quietly, but appeared to be greatly disapointed. These Indians are in most respects like those at King Georges Sound; their faces are flater and broader and their dispossions more savage but their dress and the manner of painting their foreheads is exactly the same; they have a slit thro the lower part of their under lips parallel to their mouth and two thirds the length of it, thro' which they wear a smoth white bone by way of ornament. It is about an inch and a half long, and half an inch broad; is flat and has a hook on the upper end by which it hangs upon the lip, being part seen above and part below having a very odd appearance. In rainy weather they wear a kind of frock or jacket made of the entrails of the whale or seal sewn together with sinews so close as not to admit a drop of water; of these they have two sorts, one being as thin as the skin of a bladder and the other as thick as the leather we use for gloves, they tie close round the neck and wrists and reach almost to their knees. We purchased several and found them very convenient. Their Arms and fishing gear are likewise the same as at King Georges Sound, but their Canoes are very different and of two kinds: the large open ones[1] are framed or ribbed with wood somewhat like our cutters, and covered with whale skin, instead of plank and will carry 15 or 20 men; the small ones[2] are long and narrow and sharp at both ends, they are framed with wood and entirely covered with a white skin of some fish except one or two round holes that are left open just large enough for a man to sit in. Those with only one have it in the middle and carry only one person; those with two holes have them one third of the length of the Canoe from one another and that distance from the extremities, and carry two people. They use a long paddle which is broad and flat towards the ends and narrows in the middle where they hold it in both hands, using it first on one side then on the other, in which manner they go very swiftly.

After three days stay in this cove we weighed early in the morning and stood to the northward keeping over to the east shore; at noon having a light wind and calms we were very near being carried by a small drain of a tide upon some rocks which lie above water off the point of an Island but luckily, with the assistance of our boats in towing and sounding a passage into deep water (for we had got upon a shoal) we went clear of them. In the afternoon it being quite calm we came too off an Island[3] laying at the head of the sound, about 12 Leagues from the entrance; two boats well armed with an officer in each were sent to examine an Inlet that run up to the NE; they went up 4 or 5 miles and finding it to grow much narrower returned onboard. There are two or three smaller ones along the upper part of the Sound but they did not appear to be worth searching

1 This sounds like the Eskimo *umiak.*
2 Presumably a *kayak.*
3 It is difficult to identify Gilbert's several Islands, here. They were sailing along the numerous islands on the Western side of the entrance to Prince William Sound.

into. A light breeze sprung up, we weigh'd and stood back to the southward, giving over every hope of a passage in this place. The next day we preceived another opening out to sea to the westward of that we came in at, and separated from it by a large Island laying in the entrance of the Sound which we had mistaken for the mainland. On the 21st of May we sailed through the west passage having been in here 9 Days.[1]

From hence we stood along the Coast which trended to the West S West having a very barren appearance, there being not the least Shrub to be seen. From the 24th to the 29th we were turning up to the entrance of a large inlet about 8 Leagues wide with a cluster of small Islands and rocks laying off the middle of it; it lies in Latitude 49°N and Longitude 260°E and afforded a very flattering prospect. We found a strong tide here running at the rate of 4 and half miles an hour which ebbed and flowed equal time; had soundings from 20 to 30 fathoms. The wind being directly against us we worked up with the flood and came to on the ebb, both night and day having no darkness. Found the Inlet to run up to the NNE and continued nearly the same width: the East shore is low and marshy for six or seven leagues inland and then rises into high mountains covered with snow; the West side is likewise low towards the water but not above one or two leagues in land, and in some places only one or two miles. There are two very high mountains on this side about 30 Leagues from the entrance upon one of which is a volcano and oposite them lies a small high Island. Over on the same shore the low land was quite clear of snow but with the least signs of fertility, not having a single shrub upon it. Four or five small Canoes came off to us with one or two men in each and brought with them a few fresh salmon which we purchased and heartily wished for more, these serving only to raise our desires for what

Cook
Inlet

1 Although Gilbert's dates do not exactly tally here with Cook's, he is clearly describing the eleven disappointing days they spent exploring Cook inlet, from May 26 to June 11. Earlier maps of the area had suggested that Alaska was a large island, and Cook was still hoping to find a channel through here to the mainland coast at Latitude 65°, where his search for a NW passage could begin.

we could not procure as they did not come off to us again. They were like the Natives of the sound we left both in their persons and dress, but seemingly of a more mild dispossition. Had soundings here from 25 to 20 fathoms shoaling to 15 and 10 on each side. After having worked up to the Latitude of 61°N and upwards of 60 Leagues from the entrance we found what we now preceived to be a large River to seperate into two branches, one running up to the North the other to the East, which entirely destroyed every hope of a passage. The latter we attempted to go up with the ships but found a barr with only one fathom of water across the mouth of it, which was about two miles wide with an high bluff point on each side: There is a probability of this Branch having communication with Prince William Henry Sound from which it is not far distance. Sent two boats armed with the Master to the Northward to examine the other arm of the River, the entrance of which was about a league broad with low swampy ground on each side of it. They went up 4 or 5 Leagues and finding it grow rather narrower they returned onboard.

We landed upon a small Island lying between the two branches and took possession of the Country in the name of His Britannic Majesty. About a dozen of the Natives were present and behaved very friendly but had no idea what we were doing; there are a few small pines growing here upon the low land but none betwixt this and the entrance. June 1778

Finding nothing more could be done here and having no time to spare we worked down again in the same manner as we did in coming up, for the wind unfortunately just at the time shifted round to the Southward directly against us. About a ⅓ of the way down having a modrate breeze and then about half Ebb, the ship ran aground against the edge of a shoal over upon the west shore where she remained fast. We carried out an anchor into Deep water and hove taught, and on the next flood she floated and we got her off without any damage the shoal being fine sand. This part of the Country appears to be very thinly inhabitted for we saw no more of the Natives than those that we mentioned. About the 7th of June we got out of the River which bears the name of our Commander having had very fine weather all the time we was in it. We continued to turn up the coast which from this trends to the southward to the Lat: 57°N and then turns off West having several small Islands lying off the shore at a little distance; in the Long: 204° East we had a thick fog wherein we run for a day and a night without seeing the Land for the space of 20 Leagues. The weather clearing up we saw two or three high Islands to the southward of us about 10 Leagues distance from the shore; having passed within them we had light air and calms for four or five days, where in we got but a little distance. A fair wind coming, we stood thro' a narrow passage between a large cluster of small Islands and the mainland. Two of the Natives came onboard here and gave us a letter which we could not understand but supposed it to have been left here by the Russians as we afterwards learnt to be the case. These Islands were seen by Behring and called by him **Shumagin**; they lie in Lat: 55° North and Long: 200° East and are 120 leagues distant from Cooks River. We continued to follow the direction of the Coast which trended to the WSW and passed several patches of rooks laying within us at 4 or 5 miles distance from the shore. About the 21st of June we were becalmed for two or three days off a low Island lying near the main in Lat: 54½°N and Long: 197° East to which we gave the name of Halibut, from the great quantities of that fish we caught here alongside with hook and line; they were a most welcome acquisition to us and afforded an excellent feast for 4 or 5 days. There are four very large mountains on this part of the coast nearly at equal distances from one another. But the land round them is of a very modrate height; the wester most is the highest we have seen during the voyage and perhaps in the world. It is exceeding steep all round the sides raising in a direct line and terminates in a point at the top on which is a vulcano with a large column of smoak continually issuing out of it. Yet!

Shumagin Islands

it is covered with snow all the way up. A fair wind springing up we stood to the SW and passed to the southward of several small Islands lying off the land; in the evening a thick fog coming on we hauld our wind off shore; at 4 o'clock in the morning we bore away again to the Westward with a fresh breeze tho' the fog was still so thick that we scarce could see the length of the ship from us. About an hour afterward going then 5 or 6 knots we all at once heard breakers close to us, but even in the space of a minuit we perceived by the sound that we had passed them. Hove the lead and finding ground in 20 fathom we instantly let go the anchor and took in our sails; the fog did not clear away till 10 o'clock when tho' we were lying very safe, yet, we could not help being struck with horror at the sight of the dangers we had escaped, having 3 or 4 patches of rocks above water about a ⅓ of a mile from one another on one side of us and the land half a mile distance on the other. So that even after clearing the rocks, had we stood on only six minutes longer we should have run on shore; and from the rate of our going must inevitably have been lost; a more providential escape from instant destruction being scarce to be met with.

We now weighed and turned up to a small opening to the NW which we reached in two or three days; the wind coming favourable we attempted to stand up it, but after we had got up about two miles, we found ourselves set astern by a strong current which obliged us to come to an anchor, it running at the rate of six knots. We now preceived this to be a small strait about a mile wide and 4 or 5 miles long between two Islands, lying close to a point of the main, with the Sea to the Northward of them. About an hour afterwards we weighed and stood into an excellent harbour on the SW side in Lat: 54°N Long: 193°E. The entrance into it is about a third of a mile broad with a patch of Rocks on each side, it runs up to the Southward a mile and an half and then turns off to the westward a mile further and is about half a mile wide all the way up. The shore on the east side and half up the west, is steep and Rocky; at the

English Bay

The Aleutian Islands

head of it is a black sandy beach and a large Rivulet of excellent water, which runs thro' a long narrow valley between two ridges of high hills and emptys itself here. There is likewise a Rivulet on the west side, and a fall of water from the cliffs a little above the entrance; we came to in 12 fathom water, good ground, about half way up; from whence the soundness decreased gradually to within half a mile of the head of the harbour, which is very shoal. Stedied with a small anchor and an hawser; and immediately began watering which we compleated here. The shore had a very steril appearence not having a tree of any kind upon it, only here and there a few small bushes with a blossom upon them resembling that of the apple both in colour and smell but much smaller. We were visited by the Natives[1] who ventured to come along side and onboard without the least diffidence, and behaved with the greatest civility imaginable, being more mild in their dispossion and inofencive in their behaviour than any Indians we met with on the coast, which is fully expressed in their Countinances. In their stature and complexion they resemble those of Prince William Henrys sound, but their dress is some what different; for instead of furs their garments are made of skins of other animals or those of Birds, or fish sewed together, which are generally very Dirty. They wear upon their heads a kind of wooden Bonnet without a crown to it, which they used to pull off to us and bow at the same time, as we do to one another in Europe: we supposed them to have learnt this from some Russians who probably trade to these parts. They likewise wear in rainy weather a frock made of the Intrails of fish as has been described at the last Sound; and have a slit along their underlip, and a small white bone thro' it the same as the other. They are the most tacit set of people we ever met with; for we never heard them speak but when real occasion required. Their Canoes are all of the same kind, and exactly like those we saw

1 These people were Aleuts; their culture was a variation of the Eskimo type, confined to Alaska and the Aleutian islands.

Resolution And *Discovery* In The Ice Near The Arctic Circle

Native Dance At Tonga

(Above) Portrait Of Captain Cook
(Centre Pages) Death Of Captain Cook In Kealakekua Bay, Hawaii

Queen Charlotte's Sound, New Zealand

Portrait Of Poetua, Tahitian Princess

Nootka Sound, Canada

last; the upper part of them is almost covered with darts for fishing like those described at King Georges Sound; but we did not preceive that these people had any Bows and Arrows as they have there. Their houses are different to any we have hitherto seen; and a person unaquainted with them would not suppose they were such till he came close to them, for they appear only like so many heaps of earth covered with Turf rising gradually all round to the height of three or 4 feet in the middle, where there is a hole, thro' which the Natives decend by a ladder to the floor, which is about six feet below the level of the ground and is either oblong, square or circular; and generally about 25 feet from one extremity to the other. Round the sides are placed several upright pieces of wood to support the lower part of the Roof which is one or two feet above the ground, and consists of a number of Spars laid across and meeting in the centre where they raise about two feet and rest upon a large piece of timber standing upright in the middle of the floor. Upon these spars they lay small sticks, then dryed grass and upon that a sufficient quantity of earth and turf to keep out the wet; the inside is thought remarkably dirty and contains three or four families who are separated from each other somewhat like horses in a stable, their bed places are built up round the sides, and covered with skins, and serve for seats in the day, being the only ones they have. Where they procure the wood their houses are built with we cant determine, for we are certain that there is none upon this Island; and the nearest that we have seen, is at Prince William Henrys sound, which is 250 Leagues distant; therefore I suppose it to be what has drifted along the coast which probably they go in search of. Their cheif imployment seems to be in fishing as on that their sustenance principally depends; they catch halibut, salmon and trout when in Season in great quantities, and during the summer take care to dry and lay up a sufficient stock for their winter support; we could not get any fresh fish there at this time of the year, but purchased a few dryed fish from the Natives for tobacco which they are exceeding fond of, as likewise of snuff; and were the first Indians we met with that expressed the least desire for either.

After a stay here of three or four days, on the 2nd of July we
July
1778
sailed out of the Harbour; and having a fair wind, and fine weather, we stood to the Northward, and got thro' the strait, which we were not able to do before for the strength of the Current.

From hence we followed the direction of the Coast which trends back to the NE and nearly parallel to that on the other side of the straits with which it forms a long neck of Sand from 12 to 20 Leagues in breadth and 130 in Length. The weather being very foggy, we traced this part but imperfectly, sometimes not being able to see it; having got up to the Latitude
Bristol
Bay
58½° Long: 203°E the fog cleared away and we found the coast to turn off suddenly to the westward forming a large Bay with that already past, to which we gave the name Bristol. The land here is low and broken but continued to have the same barren appearance. The weather now being very fine we kept within two or three Leagues of the shore carrying Sounding from 15 to 25 fathoms for the distance of 50 Leagues to the Cape which we named Newenham in Lat: 58° 40'N and Long: 195°E; some of our Gentlemen landed here, and saw two Deer at a distance, but did not perceive any Indians. From this Cape the Coast trends due North which we traced up to the Lat: 60N at about four Leagues from the shore not being able to approach any nearer for shoal water. In coming to an anchor here we parted our best Bower cable at the clinch in bringing up, accasioned by the strength of the Tide; which runs at the rate of four or five knots per hour; but after trying two days we were lucky enough to get our anchor again, as it lay only in 7 or 8 fathom water. The land, as far as we could see from hence continued in the same direction; and finding that we could trace it no further for shoal water we attempted to stand to the westward, directly offshore but were prevented by a shoal lying

without us; we now preceived that we had come up a channel from 3 to 6 or 7 miles wide, with a patch of rocks in the middle of it. Even with the water and a shoal on each side that the ships could not get over but so deep as to be intirely hid. Therefore we had nothing to guide us in working back to the southwards for the distance of 16 Leagues but our soundings which were about 15 fathom in mid channel. During this we were very fortunate in having modrate weather: for if in this dangerous and critical situation a gale of wind had come on added to the strength of the tide, in all probability we should have been wrecked. After having got clear of the shoals we left the coast and stood to the westward carring soundings from 38 to 22 fathom all the way to an Island[1] we fell in with on the 29th of July, in Lat: 60½° North, Long: 187° East and about 112 Leagues to the West N West of Cape Newenham. It is about three Leagues in length and two in breadth, is entirely barren and frequented only by a great number of sea birds of various kinds from which we gave it the name of Bird Island. From hence we sailed NE by N and carried the same soundings for the distance of 100 Leagues, till we made the coast again.

On the 4th of August in Lat: 64½°N and Long: 193½° East off here we lost Mr. William Anderson our surgeon, who died of a decline[2] being the second person since we left England. The first who was a quartermaster died off Sandwich Islands of the same disorder.

August 1778

The weather being very foggy we came to an anchor within a small high Island laying close to the main, where Capt Cook and some Gentlemen went onshore and gave it the name of Sledge Island from part of one they found upon it; they brought onboard a few vegitables, which we had boiled in our peas; but did not preceive any Natives here. The next day we weighed and stood along shore which trended due west but having foggy weather and a strong tide we were frequently obliged to come to

1 St Matthew Island.
2 Anderson had been ill with tuberculosis for over a year.

an anchor, after Tracing the land which is very high and barren
for the distance of 40 Leagues. In the above direction we found
it to turn off to the NNE and ending in a long sandy point with
breakers running off it; upon which we very narrowly escaped
being drove by a hard gale of wind attended with severe squalls.

This is the Western extremity of America[1], and with a point
oposite to it on the Coast of Asia called the Zerd Thamen[2] by
the Russians forms a strait between the two Continents about
14 Leagues wide, in Lat: 69° 40′N and Long: 191° East; the
first and I believe the only one that had sailed thro' it was
Behring in 1728 after whom it is named.

The gale abated after 6 or 8 hours. We left the coast and
stood over to two small Islands[3] in sight of it to the westward
which lie directly in the middle of the straits. We past close
by them they being bold too and carried soundings from 23 to
80 fathom over to the coast of Asia which we made the next
morning in Lat: 65½° North Long: 189° East. The interiour
parts are very hilly, the shore of a modrate height but is steep
and rockey and has a very sterile appearance, not having a tree
or shrub of any kind upon it that we could perceive. We came to
anchor off a small bay, the water up it being too shoal for the
ships. It is called by the Russians St. Lawrence and lies about
12 Leagues to the SW of the Straits; a few of the Natives
came off to us who are much like those of the Harbour we left in
their stature and persons, but far neater in their dress, which
consist of skins worn nearly in the same manner; they are the
only people we have seen since that time, and are called by the
Russians the Tckutski.[4] Capt Cook went onshore here with two

1 Cook named this Cape Prince of Wales.
2 Gilbert seems here to be referring mistakenly to Cape Serdtse Kamen, which is
  further North. The Easternmost point of Siberia across the Bering Strait from
  Cape Prince of Wales is Cape Dezhneva.
3 The Diomede Islands.
4 Chukchi, a Mongoloid people quite distinct from Eskimo. The Russian fur trade
  later benefitted from Cook's friendly contact with these people, who naturally
  took these Europeans to be Russians, and found them to be much kinder than the
  'bush telegraph' had led them to believe!

boats well armed and was received by a great number of them in a very friendly manner having at the same time weapons in their hands, which to appearance they designed to use only on the defensive. They made the Captain a present of several things that they had about them and would not take anything in return till after much persuasion; when the boats returned onboard we weighed and stood to the NE towards the Zard Kamen which is the Eastern extremity of Asia. Passed between it and the two Islands above mentioned and were becalmed about two days. About four or five Leagues to the Northward of them we had the same sound up as before and no particular tide or current that I recolect of any consequence. A breeze springing up, we stood over to the coast of America just to the Northward of the low point that forms that side of the straits from which we traced in a NE direction up to the Lat: 67° North where having a thick fog we stood on without seeing the land, for the space of 10 Leagues. The weather clearing up we got sight of it again and stood on to the Northward (the coast trending N by E) to the Lat: 68°; the weather than coming on foggy again, we lost sight of it and stood on to the Northward for the distance of 14 Leagues where we fell in with it and traced it on a N by W direction up to 70° from whence it trends to the NE. This part of the Coast is high inland but rather low towards the shore, and is thought intirely covered with Snow. Having got up to the Lat: 70° 40' North Long: 198½° and NE by N 110 Leagues from the straits, we found that we could not approach the Land within 6 or 8 Leagues for shoal water or get any further[1] to the North for a firm field of Ice, which extended from the shore as far to the westward as we could see. We now left the coast and stood along the Ice keeping as close to the firm body as we could and passed thro' a great number of loose fields laying off it; having run in this manner about 45 Leagues we got clear of it and found an open sea to the north of us; we

The Arctic Sea

1 They were turned back by the Arctic ice-pack on August 18, at their most Northerly point of 70° 44'. The nearest land was Icy Cape.

still continued our Course to the WSW and did not meet with it
again for the space of 36 Leagues from whence we traced it in a
firm body in the above direction for that distance till we found it
joine to the oposite coast of Asia in Lat: 68° 3'N and Long:
181° East, which is 127 Leagues from the Northermost land
seen of America, and bears NWW 100 Leagues from Behring
Straits. Had regular soundings all the way across from 28 to 32
fathoms and were often in very great danger of being emburyed
by the loose Ice from having thick hazing weather all the time
we were amongst it. During this cold and disagreeable passage
we met with great numbers of sea horses[1] but why they are so
called I can't imagine, for they bear not the smallest
resemblence to that animal. They are about the size of a large
Ox and have a thick hide thinly covered with short bristly hair;
their heads are very small and is the only part about them that
has the least appearance of a beast; the rest of the body being
like a fish, the hinder parts tapering and terminating in a couple
of fins about two feet long instead of feet; having likewise one
upon each shoulder with which they swim faster than can be
imagined but move slowly upon the Ice. They have two large
white Ivory teeth like those of the Elephant projecting with a
small curve downwards from their upper jaw; which are from
one and a half to two feet in length and nearly parallel to each
other at about 5 inches distance and end in a point at the outer
extremities. That they are indowed with a greater share of
sagacity and understanding than the generality of animals will
appear from the following instance; when they went to sleep a
great number of them assembled upon a small piece of Ice
seperated from the rest and only just large enough for that
purpose, that they may the more readily get off from it into the
water in case of the approch of an enimy. I believe the only one
they are apprehensive of is the white bears which is likewise
amphibious; and being much nimbler upon the Ice than they
are, have there greatly the advantage of them, but in the water

1 Walruses.

the Sea horse is the swiftist and most formidable on account of its teeth. Therefore to prevent being surprized in their sleep they always appoint one as a sentinall and place it in the middle to keep watch over them during that time which charge is strictly and faithfully performed keeping the foreparts of its body erect, and an attentive eye alround. As we approached them with the ships they would lie very quiet till we came within two cables length of them, when the one that had the watch would make a great noise to allarm the rest upon which they all began by degrees to raise their heads and shoulders and look around them and then crawl to the edge of the Ice and plunge head foremost into the water; so that by the time we had got within a ½ a cable length of them there would not be one remaining; the noise they make is a mean betwixt the barking of a dog and the bellowing of an Ox. We hoisted out our boats to get some and with great difficulty killed and brought onboard 8 or 10 of them for altho' we rowed ever so softly, yet! by the time we got within good musket shot it was a great chance if there were any left; and unless we fired at them upon the Ice it was twenty to one that we could hit them in the water, as they dive immediately. They will in generall bear three or four balls in their bodies before they are killed except in their heads and there one is sufficient. Their affection for their young and even for one another is very great and remarkable, for whenever one of them got wounded in the water if any of the rest were near they would come to it assistance and carry it off if possible at the risk of their own lives; but if by chance we had killed one of their young the Mother would come and make every attempt to rescue it from us and even try to upset the boat it was in, by hooking the boatside with her teeth which she would follow till she was killed; all the time making a lamentable noise and shewing every sign of real parental distress.

After we had got them onboard they were skinned and cut up by the butcher. The hides we preserved for the Rigging, the Blubber or fat we put into casks to melt down into train oil for

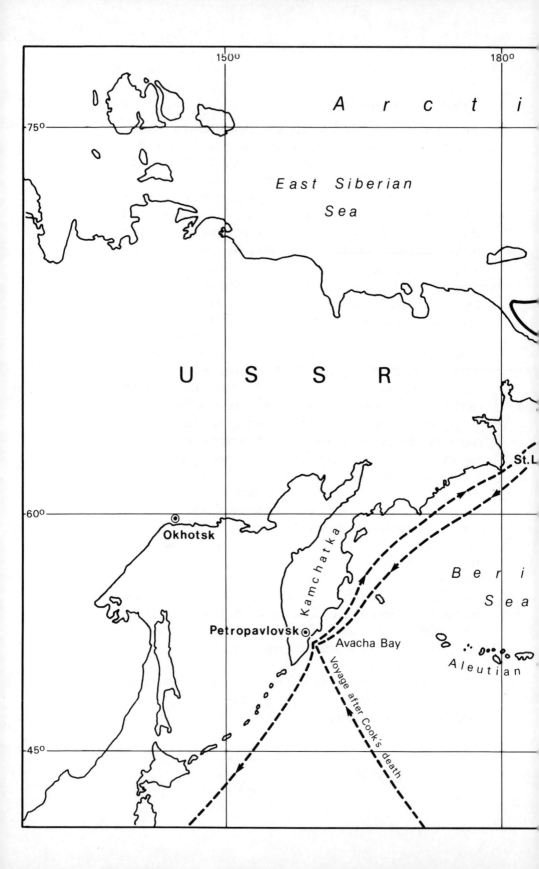

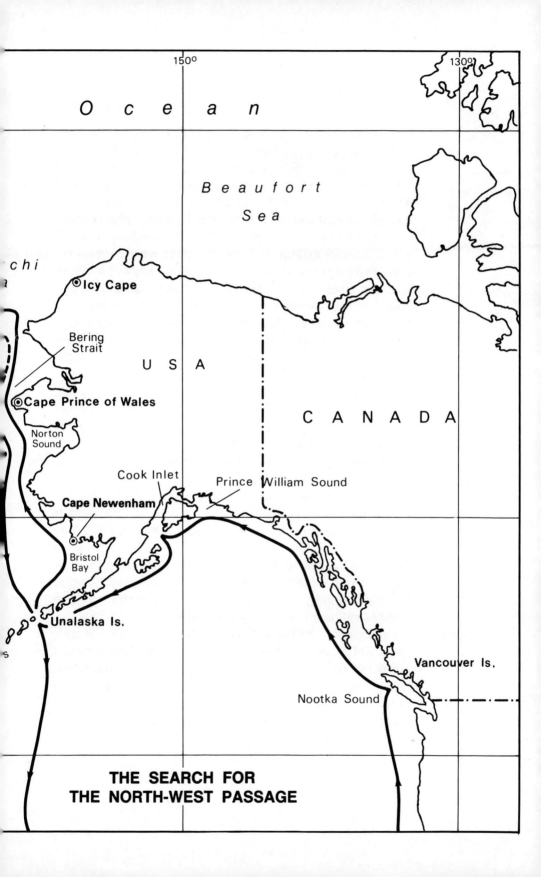

THE SEARCH FOR
THE NORTH-WEST PASSAGE

our lamps; and the flesh disgustfull as it was we eat thro'
extreme hunger, caused by the badness of our provisions and
short allowance, which were but just enough to exist upon and
were now reduced on account of this supply: the quality of
which will be best described in the several preperations it went
through before it was possible to eat it. In the first place we let it
hang up for one day that the blood might drain from it, which
would continue to drop for four or five days, when permitted to
remain so long but that our hunger would not allow of it at first;
after that we towed it overboard for 12 hours then boiled it four
hours and the next day cut it into steaks and fryed it; and even
then it was too rank both in smell and tast to make use of except
with plenty of pepper and salt and these too articles were very
scarce amongst us; however our hunger got the better of the
quality and in the quantity. We found some comfort having as
much of it as we could eat which was what we had been along
time unaccustomed to. We salted some of it by way of
experiment which after laying two or three weeks we found was
a little improved but still could only be eat by such as were at
the point of perishing with hunger and were no other food was
to be secured. Having made the coast of Asia as before
mentioned, we found it to trend to the SE. It is of a modrate
height and appears at a distance like a number of small Islands
but on a nearer approach we preceived it to be a straight shore
without the least signs of an inlet, or Harbour, and having a
very barren appearence, there not being a tree or shrub to be
seen; we kept close in with it in the above direction down to
Behring Streights, which we stood thro' and having very fine
weather still continued along that shore.

September
1778

After passing the Bay of St. Lawrence we traced it SW by S
about 30 Leagues and then bore away for the Coast of America
and in two Days on the 8th of September, made Sledge Island,
being now about 5 weeks since we left it. As we had not
explored that part of the coast which lay to the Eastward of us,
we now traced it due East for the distance of 30 Leagues, when

we preceived land to the Southwards forming with that we were standing along; a large sound to which we gave the name of Norton. We had very pleasant weather here, but the wind shifted directly against us; however we worked up to the Eastward along the North Shore for several Leagues till we could not proceed any further for shoal water. Having carried sounding from 4½ to 3½ fathoms for a very considerable distance we came to an anchor off a large sandy beach, there being not the least appearance of a harbour on this part of the Coast which is very mountains inland; but toward the shore is of a modrate height and thinly covered with small pines. This being the first wood we had seen since we left Cooks River, it was quite a new sight to us and appeared very delightfull. We found Hurtle and Crane berries here in great plenty which proved a far more delicious treat to us than the fruits of the tropical Islands, being at present in much greater want of them; yet! we got but few as we were allowed to go on shore only for a very short time. We took in some water here and a great quantity of wood, the beach being almost covered with old trees and branches that had drifted upon it. As we could not get any further with the two ships two boats were sent, well armed, under the command of Mr King our second Lieut to examine the head of the sound and discover if the land on the south side joined to this on the North. We saw about 12 of the Natives from whom we purchased several salmon trout which were very acceptable to us. After three days we weighed and stood over to the other side of the Sound which is here about 7 Leagues across and anchored within a bluffpoint that stretched a little way out and formed a small Bay to the Westward of it; we landed and found great plenty of berries, and a few currant bushes but they had no fruit left upon them. We gathered great quantities of an Herb that grows here to make use of in lieu of tea, which has a very agreeable flavour; and is the same kind as is used by the Indians of Hudsons Bay, and Newfoundland. We only saw one copse of trees here; the shore on this side being in

Norton
Sound

general quite low and marshy. After three days absence the
boats returned onboard having been up seven or 8 Leagues; but
could not reach the head of the Sound within two Leagues for
shoal water, they found the land on each side to meet within a
small space of no consequence. The next day we weighed and
stood to the Westward along the south shore, but could not
approach it for shoals. After running 10 or 12 Leagues we
hauled round a small low Island lying close to the main which
from hence trends round to the Southward; we attempted to
trace it along but were again prevented by shoal water, not
having been able to get near enough to keep sight of the land.
This part of the Coast which makes the South point of the
Sound lies in Lat: 63°N Long: 197° East being due North and
63 Leagues distance from that part above Cape Newenham,
which we were obliged to leave for the same reasons: so that the
above space remains still unexplored but the shoal water to the
Southward and Northward of it leaves not the least room for a
safe passage there. On the 26th of Sept we left the land and
stood to the Westward, and on the 28th we fell in with an
Island In Lat: 63¼° and Long: 191° East; the weather being
foggy we could not see the extent of it and the wind blowing
very fresh, we did not stop but stood to the Southward for Bird
Island, which we made and from thence directed our course to
the SSE for the Harbour we left on the 2nd of July, which is
144 Leagues distance.

October
1778 We arrived[1] there the 3rd of October and mored the ships
about ½ way up, and as we intended to stay some time to
refresh ourselves we set up our observatories, to make observa-
English
Bay,
Unalaska tions to regulate our timekeeper which we had not done since we
left King Georges Sound. We likewise sent our sails and empty
casks onshore to repair them. Hurtle and Crane berries we found
in great quantities, and the small bushes that were in blossom
when we sailed were now full of black berries about the size of a

---

1 Samgoonoodha Harbour, which the Russians later called English Bay, in
  Unalaska.

large currant; they were very agreeable to the taste, and of a different kind from any we had ever seen but did not continue above a week or ten days after we came in, being nearly out of season.

The Natives came and traided with us as before in a very freindly manner; they have got six or seven small villages in different parts of the Island which is about 12 Leagues in extent but they dont appear to be very numerous. During the first week we caught plenty of salmon trout with our seine by spreading it opposite to the Rivulet of fresh waters, there being several that empty themselves here; we likewise sent a boat every day without the Harbour to fish with hook and line which generally returned with a sufficient quantity of Halibuts to serve the whole ships company; these few refreshments we found very comfortable having been without any kind for a long time. After we had been in about eight days one of the Natives brought the Captain a present of a cake made of Rye Flower with some Salmon baked in the middle of it, and told us it came from some people upon the Island about five Leagues distant; Cpt Cook immediately supposed them to be Russians who had either settled there, or were traiding upon the Island; therefore he sent one of our Corporal of Marines (who was a very intelligent man) back with the Native to learn who they were. In two days time he returned with three Russians; from whome we were informed that about fifteen of them had settled there and lived together, in a house built of logs of wood laid horizontally one upon another and let in at the corners. About three days afterwards we were visited by the cheif person amongst them,[1] who was Capt. of a small one masted sloop, they had got laid up there, which was remarkable clumsey and ill built; he seemed to be very active and Intelligent but unluckily we had no person onboard who had the least knowledge of the Rusian language; therefore we were obliged to convers with him principally by signs. He understood figures

Unalaska

1 Gerassim Gregoriev Ismailov.

and likewise our charts, exceedingly well, and informed us that
there were a range of small Islands extending from this, about 6
or 8 degrees to the Westward and that they had some small
settlements there; he gave us a manuscrip chart of them and
those parts of the continent that he was aquainted with, which
was tollerably corect, and we learnt from him that they had
extended their traid along the coast to the Eastward as far as
Shumagin Islands which lie 84 Leagues from hence; and was
the place where the Natives brought of a letter to us that we
could not understand. He likewise informed us that some
Rusians had attempted to settle upon the main, about Norton
Sound, but were not able to accomplish it, having had some of
their people cut off by the Natives who were too numerous for
them tho' we saw very few thereon. Capt Cook made him a
present of a Quardrent with which he was much pleased; and
seemed to understand the use of it very well, though they have
got none in these parts. We enquired of him concerning the
state of their settlements in the Bay of Awatcha on the Coast of
Kamchatka which he told us was very well peopled and had a fort
with 40 guns in it; and when we acquainted him that we should
go there he gave us a letter for the Governor, and said that it
would by no means answer our purpose, as they would give us
no assistance or supplies of any kind, and endevoured much to
presuade us from it. They had seen us the first time we came
here, but were then affraid to come near us, not knowing our
intentions or who we were; and even now we could not
perfectly satisfy them, with respect to the latter as they had
little of no knowledge of the English, or any other European
state but their own. They differ very little from the Natives in
their dress, or yet in their sustenance except in having a small
quantity of Rye flower that they get from the Bay of Awatcha
which lies 410 Leagues to the Westward. The whole intention
and support of their settlements upon these Islands consists in
skins and furs, part of which they traid for and part exact from
the Natives as a tribute to the Empress. The mild dispossion of

these Indians which we took notice of the first time we was here, is now very easily accounted for as they are all subjected to the Russians who keep them in awe with their fire arms.

The name they give to the Harbour we were in is Samganooda, and to the Island Oonalaska [Unalaska] which with the Island of Oomenak that lies to the NE of it, forms the small strait between them that we came thro' when we were here before; the latter lies close to the point of a long neck of Land before mentioned, which we find from their charts is called Alaska.

Having overhauld our Rigging, completed our water and refreshed ourselves as well as the place would admit of; again after a stay of above three weeks we weighed and stood thro' the strait to the Westward to examine some Islands lying in that direction, which the Rusian Capt. had informed us of; but the weather coming on foggy and a very hard gale of wind directly against us we were obliged to give up our design and bear away again for the strait; which we stood through and on the 31st of October 1778 we lost sight of the Land, and directed our course to the Southward for Sandwich Islands where we intended to pass the winter; Capt Cook, having publickly declared to the people upon leaving the Ice that he intended to make another attempt there in search of a passage the next summer.

This ended a very hazardous and disagreeable Season; wherein we surveyed an extent of Coast of 1200 Leagues which is far more than ever any navigator had done before. It is necessary to observe that having very often had either a tide or current when near the shore we were frequently obliged to come to anchor, but as to have mentioned it every time would have been too tedious. I have only taken notice of the most material ones especially the gales we had after leaving King Georges Sound and the one above mentioned. We were very fortunate in Generally having fine weather for our purpose; but particularly when in any dangerous situations as we were often in such, for a considerable time together, that if a gale had then come on, we must [have] inevitably been lost.

Chapter Four

HAWAII

On leaving the Land we had a very hard gale of wind from the NW which lasted three days, but after that had fine weather all the passage. About the 23 of November, we got into the parallel of Sandwich Islands, and seven or eight degrees to the eastward of them which we did intentionally to discover if there were any more in the cluster to windward of those we had seen before. We now stood to the westward, the two ships keeping abreast of one another at two Leagues distance all the day and lying too during the night; after sailing in this manner three days, we fell in with a large Island [Maui] in Lat: 20¾°N and Long: 205½° East and about 100 Leagues from Towi [Kauai]. The interior parts are hilly but the shore is of a modrate height and has a very fertile and delightfull appearence; as soon as we had got within a mile, the Natives came off to us and ventured onboard without any hesitation and behaved very friendly; they brought with them the productions of the Island in great plenty, which we purchased along side with the usual articles.

    The joy that we experienced on our arrival here is only to be conceived by ourselves or people under like circumstances; for after suffering excess of hunger and a number of other hardships most severely felt by us for the space of near ten months, we had now come into a delightfull climate were we had almost every thing we could wish for, in great profusion; and this luxury was still heightened by our having been at a shorter

November
1778

Maui

allowance of provisions this last passage than ever we was at before. Having procured a sufficient supply to last us four or five days, we stood off and worked up along shore to the SE keeping at the distance of 5 or 6 Leagues from the Land; when our stock onboard began to grow short, we went close in and traided for more, and then stood off again; this we continued to do for 10 or 12 days till we weathered the SE point of the Island which is called by the Natives Mow:wee [Maui].

December
1778

Hawaii

From hence we stood over to a large Island called Owyhee that lies in sight of it to the SW which we made on the NE side. It is very mountainous in land, and the shores in general steep; but exceeding fertile. The Natives came off to us in great numbers and behaved in a very friendly manner; we traided with them as usual till we had purchased provisions enough for five or six days, which we did in three or four hours and might have got three times as much if we had chose, for the greater part of their Canoes were obliged to return to the shore with what they had brought off to us. We then stood off about 5 or 6 Leagues from the Land and worked up along shore, to the SE keeping at that distance till our stock was expended; and then went in and traided for more, as we had done off the other Island. As we were not yet in want of water Capt Cook prefered this method of passing the time to going into a harbour as it was a great means of saving traid, of which he was apprehensive we should not have as much as we might have accasion for. The Discovery having broke an arm off one of her Bower Anchors at the Island of Desolation, the armourors were employed while we lay in Sumganooda Harbour in working it up; for that [we obtained] paw paw which was proportionably divided betwixt the two ships and [that] with several spare iron stores, principally belonging to the shallope, served us for Trade during our stay among the Islands.

January
1779

After standing off and on for upwards of a month, and having coasted along near ⅔ of the Island we began to be in want of water; therefore the master with two boats well armed we sent inshore to look for a harbour, and very luckily found a small bay opposite to us which was the first we had seen the least appearance of. But however as this could not be preceived till we came within two miles of it; we were inclined to think we probably might have passed others of the same kind. The next morning being about the 16 of January we stood in for it, with a light breeze, and as we approached near the shore we were surrounded with upwards of 1,000 Canoes at the mean rate of six people in each and so very anxious were they to see us, that those who had none swam off in great numbers, and remained along side in the water, both men, women and children for four or five hours, without seeming tired; the decks both above and below were entirely covered with them, so that when we wanted to work the ship we could not come at the ropes without first driving the greatest part of them overboard; which they bore with the utmost cheerfullness and good nature jumping from every part of her into the water, as fast as they could, appearing to be much diverted at it, and would come onboard again when the business was over.

This Bay is situated on the west side of the Island and in Lat: 19½°N and Long: 204°E, and is called by the Natives Carria cotah [Kealakekua]. It is small and open to the sea which causes a great swell to set in, and a great surf breaking on the shore; renders the Landing rather difficult the Bottom of it, is a high steep Cliff; but the sides are low and level; with a Town upon each; at least eight times as big as any we had seen before in the south sea. The Country here is one entire plantation; as far as we could see from the ship which is devided into squares by stones thrown together or hedges of sugar cane. We moored with the Bowers, in 10 fathom of water gravel bottom about ⅔ of a mile from the Town on the North side, and ⅓ from a low sandy beach on the South side, near the bottom of the Bay; which is the only one in it.

We got our observatories and tents onshore here as usual and pitched them upon a large oblong piece of ground walled

Kealakekua Bay

round with stones,[1] two or three feet high which was held sacred by the Natives, who notwithstanding their curiosity, so great was their superstition, that none but the chiefs dare even venture to come upon it so that our people were the less disturbed by them. The sailmakers were sent onshore with the greatest part of our sails to repair them. They being now very much worn; as was all our rigging which we carefully overhauled here.

We were surrounded everyday with a great number of Canoes and supplied by the Natives with provisions, in the most plentifull and hospitable manner imaginable. The King of the Island whos name was Terriaboo[2] and several other powerfull chiefs, frequently came onboard to visit Capt Cook, who always received them with the greatest respect. They generally brought with them a large present of Hogs, Fowls, Fruit, and for which in return he gave them at different times four or five small Iron Daggers, about two feet and a half long, in form of their own wooden ones and made by the armourer for that purpose; likewise such other trinkets as they were pleased with. What we was most in search of here was good water, that which there is being in standing pools, and very muddy and brakish, except some we got from a small spring in a well, at the foot of a rock close to the beach which yielded very little, and tho' it was clear and much better than the other yet! it was rendered brackish from its being so near the waterside. We purchased not less than 10 or 12 puncheons of excellent salt here; which is [principle] made by the sun, and was the first we met with during the voyage. This proved a very welcome supply; as it enabled us to salt down pork for sea, which otherwise we could not have done having used all we had onboard for that purpose at Otaheite.

February 1779

One of our seamen died here, whom we interred onshore in one of their burying places. Capt Cook read prayers over him in

1 The shore party worked next to (but not in) a walled *heiau* or open air temple.
2 Gilbert's version of the name of the powerful chief Kalani'opu'u.

the usual manner, and the Natives, who were present on the occasion, according to their custom threw a couple of small pigs and some fruit into the grave, which were covered up with him. The latter part of the time we lay in Matavai Bay in Otaheite and at Amsterdam, one of the Friendly Islands, being five weeks at each; we found supplies of all kinds began to grow scarce but that was far from being the case here, for everything was as plentifull the last Day, as when we first came in. Having got everything off from the shore, in the evening about seven o'clock we preceived the house to be on fire that our sailmakers had worked in, which we were in general of opinion they did on purpose thro' some superstitious notion they had among them.

It being now about the 23rd of February[1] and the season[2] approaching, after a stay of near a month, we sailed from the Bay with an intention of going to the West ward to these Islands we had been at before to take in a supply of yams for sea, as they had none here; but in this we were unfortunately prevented, for after working up along shore to the Northward a considerable distance against a very strong breeze, we discovered a spring in the head of our foremast right a thwart from one cheek to the other which obliged us to put back to Carriaco'ah Bay, to repair it; and having a fair wind for it we got in the next Day and moored as before.

We immediately began to unrigg the ship as far as was necessary and having raised a pair of sheers with two Main Top masts, we got out the fore mast which was hauled up upon the beach to be repaired and the carpenters of both ships were sent onshore for that purpose. The place our tents were pitched upon before being close to the beach we set them up again on the same spot; for the people who were to work upon the mast and Mr King our Lieut. was ordered to superintend this duty with a guard of about 8 Marines for their protection. The

1 This is an inexplicable dating error. The ships left Kealakekua Bay (for the first time) on February 4.
2 That is, the few summer months of the far North.

observatories were likewise sent onshore with the Astronomical Instruments; and several of our sails to repair having
split them while we were out.

The Natives did not appear to receive us this time with that
Friendship that they had done before. Our quick return seemed
to create a kind of Jealousey amongst them with respect to our
intentions; as fearing we should attempt to settle there, and
deprive them of part if not the whole of their Country. This idea
Capt Cook took every method to remove by telling and shewing
them the reason that obliged us to come in again with which
they apparently seemed to be very well satisfied. The third day
we had been here in the afternoon one of the Natives onboard
the Discovery stole a pair of Tongs from off the Armourers forge,
and got into his Canoe with them. The alarm being given,
several of them began to paddle away as fast as they could;
upon this the Master and a Midshipman and two men instantly
got into their Jolly boat and without any arms, persued the
Canoe they suspected, which reached the shore long before
them; and the men had got out and hauled it upon the beach
where several others were lying. The master and midshipman
landed amongst a great number of the Natives and were going
to seize one of the Canoes when a chief who was present told
them that it belonged to him and they could not have it; and
indeed it was, very probably, but they mistook the one the man
got into who committed the Theft, either in pushing off from the
ship, amongst so many, or in hauling up; but they still foolishly
persisted in attempting to take it away. The Chief layed hold of
them and gave them a severe beating with his hands, which the
two men, who remained in the Jolly boat perceiving, they
rowed off to a little distance and got clear. Our pinnace, that was
laying not far off waiting for Capt Cook with only the crew in
her, who seeing the affair went without any orders to their
assistance; but as soon as they came near the shore the Natives
lay hold of the Boat and hauled her up high and dry upon the
beach, and broke some of the oars, which obliged the crew to

take to the water and swim to the Jolly boat, the Indians at the same time pelting them with stones. In a little time they were quiet and called to the people in the boat to come onshore and that they would let them have the pinnace; which they did with the oars that remained and likewise released the Master and midshipman. About an hour afterwards Capt Cook hearing of the quarrel was very angry and gave our people a severe repremand for their rashness; he walked round with one of the Officers to the place where it happened and found every thing very peaceable.

The next morning which was the 14th of Feb. 1779, at daylight the Discovery found her six oard cutter missing, that had been moored at the buoy, which we immediately supposed to have been stolen by the Natives, inconsequence of the above quarrel. When Capt Cook was informed of it, he ordered a Boat from each ship well armed to row off the mouth of the Bay to prevent the Canoes from going out, and if any attempted it, to seize, and send them in again; at the same time, preposed to Capt Clerke for him to go onshore and indevour to preswade the King to come onboard that he might confine him till the Boat was returned according to his usual custom in these cases. But he seemed to express a desire to decline it on account of his health. Capt Cook said no more about the matter; but went himself with three boats. Viz: a six oard pinnace in which he had with him a mate the Lieut of Marines, and some of his men; a six oard Launch with the 3 Lieuts a mate some marines and a few additional seamen, and a four oard cutter with a mate and the midshipman that rowed her, being in all including the crews of the Launch and pinnace about 38 people, with each a musket a cutlass and cartridge boxes. Having landed at the Town on the North side of the Bay[1] with the Lieut of Marines, a Sergeant, Corporal, and seven privit men, he ordered the boats with the rest of the people to lie off, at a little distance, and wait for him; he then proceeded with the Marines under arms up to

1 The village of Kawaloa.

the Kings house which was about 200 yards from the water
side, where he found him with several Cheifs and not less than
two or three thousand of the Natives. After the usual
ceremonies had passed the Captain invited him to come
onboard which at first he absolutely refused but after being
pressed for some time, he seemed inclinable to consent; and [it]
was thought he would have come, had he not been prevented by
the Chiefs who would not permit Him, as in all probability they
saw into the Design. This enraged Capt Cook very much as he
was not accustomed to have his intentions frustrated by any
person; and had but little command over himself in his anger.
At this instant a canoe came over from the other side of the Bay
and brought the Natives intilligence that a Chief was killed
there by one of our boats firing on shore. Upon this they began
to arm themselves with Spears and pieces of the Branches of
trees that they broak up in a hurry instead of Clubs; and some of
the Chiefs had the same Iron Daggers that we had given them.
The Capt had with him a Doubled Barreled piece, one loaded
with small shot the other with ball and a hanger, by his side.
They now began to press together and grew rather tumultuous
and some in particular insulting him, he beat them with the butt
end of his musket which caused them to be still more so; Mr
Philips the Lieut of Marines preceiving this repeatedly told Capt
Cook of the danger he apprehended they were in, and urged
him to retire, which as if fate had determined he should fall, he
took not the least notice of; but fired at one of them with the
small shot and wounded him and a little afterwards at a chief
with ball, but misfiring him killed the man that stood next to
him out right, and altho' this enraged them to the highest degree,
yet! they then did not dare to attack him. At last finding it was
impossible to accomplish his disign, he ordered the marines to
retreat and was himself following them and possibly would
have got safe off, had not the people in the boats very
unfortunately on hearing the second report of his musket, began
to fire upon the Natives which threw them into a state of fury;

the marines likewise on shore without orders followed their example, and Capt Cook had not sooner got to the water side and waved to the boats to give over fireing, when one of the Cheifs more daring than the rest steeped behind and stabed him betwixt the shoulders with an Iron Dagger. Another at that Instant gave him a blow with a club on the head by which he fell into the water, they immediately leaped in after and keeped Him under for a few minuits, then hauled him out upon the rocks and beat his head against them several times; so that there is no doubt but that he quickly expired. The marines likewise at the same time after they had discharged their pieces were closely attacked and not being able to load again, the Corporal and three private men that could not swim, were seized and killed upon the spot. The Lieutenant, Sergeant, and the other four, leaped into the water, which was four or five feet deep close to the Rocks, and escaped to the pinnace which was laying within 30 yards of the shore, but by reason of the continual showers of stones that were thrown at them, and the confusion of those people getting in, they could not afford the least assistance to Capt Cook, and very narrowly escaped from being taken. The Launch that lay close without her, and the cutter that was inshore at a little distance both kept up a brisk fire for the space of 10 or 15 minuits till they were obliged to retire; having killed and wounded several of the Natives and caused the greatest part of them to retreat, and we were informed by the gentlemen in the Cutter who were the last that left the shore, that very few of them remained by the dead bodies when the launch and pinnace came away; and during the fireing onshore we saw a great number of the Natives running away up an ajacent hill at whom we fired five or six shots from our great guns, but our first Lieut. would not allow of any more.

When on the return of the boats informing us of the Captains Death, a general silence ensued throughout the ship for the space of near half an hour: it appearing to us somewhat like a Dream that we could not reconcile ourselves to for some time.

Greif was visible in evry Countenance; some expressing it by tears and others by a kind of gloomy dejection, more easy to be conceived than described, for as all our hopes centred in him, our loss became irrepairable and the sense of it was so deeply impressed upon our minds as not to be forgot.

Such was the confusion of the people when they came onboard that they did not preceive till a quarter of an hour afterwards how many of the marines were missing; Mr Philips the Lieut. who behaved with great prudence and courage, received a large wound upon his shoulder by a spear, and one of the private men was wounded in his cheek close below his Eye, two inches and a half of the point of a spear having broke short off and was burried in his head; the others had several bruises from the stones that were thrown at them but suffering no hurt of any consequence.

During this our people on the southside of the Bay, under the direction of Mr. King the Lieut. were very fortunately reinforced by some of our boats crew that had been rowing off the mouth of the Bay before any disturbance had began there; being then altogether about twenty four in number, tho' not above two thirds of them had muskets. On preceiving they were likely to be attacked they took possession of a burying place that lay near them, which was a large platform of earth thrown up and fenced with stones, being about 150 yards in length 60 in breadth, and the sides six or eight feet perpendicular all round, except a small passage where not more than two people could go up abreast; nothing could be more conveniently situated than this place as from thence they could not only protect the masts, tents and observatories, which lay between them and the beach and within less than a musket shot, but were secure from an encounter that they would not have been able to resist. The Natives did not venture either to make an open effort to force them from this their post or to come near the tents; but keeped up a distant and vigorous attack by heaving a great number of stones from behind the trees and houses, which lay behind them. By creeping along under cover of these walls, they were able to approach very close to the platform without being seen and when they thought themselves near enough would stand up and heave several stones, and then retire for more; this they continued, for some time and when any of them fell, another of them would stepforth and carry off the body at the risk of his own life. These Indians use a large thick mat which they hold before them by way of a sheild against their own wooden spears; and at the beginning of the attack several of them came to the edge of a pool, within reach of the shot to dip them in the water, and then would hold them up in defiance, thinking by that means to quench the fire of the muskets by which they supposed they were killed; but in that point we quickly undeceived them: the Discovery laying nearest over to this side fired several shot onshore which terrified them very much. After two or three hours they retired with the loss of six or eight killed and some wounded, finding in vain to carry on anything further against our people in their present situation and thinking, I suppose by that means to draw them from it; but they wisely kept possession of their post.

About two hours after the Death of Capt Cook we went with all the boats from both ships well manned and armed, and brought them off with the mast and every thing else we had onshore, very safe, the Natives not daring to molest us. The remainder of the forenoon we were employed in getting the mast upon the booms for the Carpenters to work at, they having done very little to it as yet.

Capt Clerke, now came onboard and took the Command of the Resolution and appointed Mr Gore our first Leiut. to that of the Discovery, and Mr Harvey one of the mates to be Lieut. in his room.

In the afternoon not withstanding what had passed, two of the Natives from the Town on the Northside of the Bay, had courage to come alongside, which was placing great confidence in us and proves the high opinion they entertain of our integrity. One of them was a priest, whom we had often before known to have behaved very trecherously therefore supposed in the present case that he had no good intentions towards us, and so highly were our people exasperated at the sight, that it was with great difficulty the officers could prevent their fireing at him. After staying about a quarter of an hour he returned to the shore, and continued to make these short visits onboard every forenoon and afternoon, for three or four days afterwards; which I believe was to see whether or not we were making any further preperations against them. Mr King now our first Lieut. was sent off the Town on the Northside with all our boats well manned and armed to treat with the Natives for the Bodies; carrying a white flag as a signal of peace for that purpose. They were assembled along the shore in great numbers with their weapons in their hands and bidding us defiance, in the most contemptous manner imaginable; for they seemed to pride themselves very much in having killed our principal Cheif, but from what we afterwards learnt they had very little reason, having lost not less than eight or ten Cheifs and about 20 common members besides several wounded, amongst whom chanced to be the greatest part of those who assisted in the murder of our people. They strove much to preswade us to land but without effect, one of them was dressed in Capt Cooks jacket and trowsers, and another had his hanger in his hand, which he kept shaking at us, and making use of every threatening and insolent gestures he could possibly invent. This enraged the sailors to the highest degree and it was with the utmost difficulty they were restrained from fireing upon them; finding we would not come any nearer, two of them ventured to swim off to us, whom we informed that we had no intentions of making an attack but came only to demand the Bodies, which to amuse us for the present they said were carried away some distant into the Country; that we could not have them then, but promised to bring them off to us in the morning; therefore preceiving they were not to be procured at that time the boats returned on board.

We were rather apprehensive that they intended to make an attack upon the ships in the night. Therefore took every necessary percaution, to prevent being surprized, by keeping our guns, and swivels loaded, a sentry forward, abaft, and on each gangway; one third of the people always under arms, and a four oared cutter well armed constantly rowing round us at a little distance while it was dark, which both ships continued to do during our stay here.

The next morning the Seamen earnestly solisited the Captain that they might go onshore with their arms to reveng the Death of their old Commander, which he did not think proper to permit; as it was not the intention of the officers to persue measures of that kind for a quarrel we had principally brought upon ourselves but preceiving they were very eagerly bent upon it, he framed an excuse to pacify them for the present by telling them, he could not possibly think of allowing it whilst the ships remained in such a defenceless state; but that in two days time when we had got things into a little order they should have the leave for that purpose. By keeping them thus in suspence for three or four days their rage began to abate: and tis well he did for had he at first positively denighed them, so highly were they incensed against the Natives, that I believe the officers would not have been able to have kept them onboard. Being rather suspicious that they were assembling canoes round the North point of the Bay, a boat with an officer was sent to see, who found no apperences of any. The forenoon a Canoe with three men in her came off from the Northside about half way to the ships, where they stopped and began to throw stones towards us; in which they could not heave half that distance. They could not have no other intention but that of insulting of us; one of them all the time very triumphantly kept waving Capt Cooks hat over his head till some muskets were fired at them, and then they instantly put back to the shore.[1]

Our cheif object at present was the Foremast which the Carpenters of both ships were working upon with the utmost expedition; making new cheeks for it out of a spare anchor stock. In the afternoon seeing a great number of the Natives assemble upon the shore on the northside of the Bay we fired a few shots at them from our great guns which quickly dispersed them.

When the old priest[2] came onboard we enquired of him concerning the Bodies, but could get no satisfactory account of them; and when we asked him why they were not brought off agreeable to the promise made yesterday he said they had been carried to different parts of the Island, and were not yet collected together but that we should have them the next day; which we preceived was only an excuse to keep us quiet. Therefore gave over every hope of having them returned as judging that they had otherwise disposed of them, and did not wish us to know in what manner.

On the 16th nothing remarkable happened till about 9 o'clock in the evening when some people were discovered paddling very softly to the ships; it being quite dark and not knowing how many there might be two or three of the sentrys instantly fired at them. Neverthe less they persisted coming towards us, and finding there was only one small canoe, we suffered her to come alongside, when to our great astonishment they proved to be two of the Natives who had brought with them about five pounds of human flesh which they told us was Capt Cooks, and that they were sent by a priest that lived on the Southside of the Bay, who had before always treated us with great hospitality. We learnt that Him and his adherents, still remained firmly attached to us, but were too few to declare it to

1 One man injured in this incident was Kamehameha, later to become the first King of Hawaii.
2 Koa.

their Countrymen, which was the reason of their coming in the dark that it might not be known. After giving them some presents, they returned to the shore, having luckily excaped being hurt in approaching the ship. This small remains of our unfortunate Commander which appeared to have been taken from the inside of his thigh, was all our friend could procure for us, and a great proof of his sincerity, but answered no good purpose to us, as the sight of it, struck every one with horror, and tended only to disquiet the sailors, by renewing their desire to be revenged of the Natives which had begun to wear off.

Beginning now to be greatly in want of water we were necessitated to go onshore again at all events, and endevour to get off a sufficiency to last us to some other place; accordingly in the morning of the 17th we sent the two launches full of casks to a small well before mentioned, on the southside close above the beach, with other boats manned and armed, to protect them. The Discovery also hauled close in for that purpose. We had not been long ashore before the Natives began to anoy us by throwing stones from behind the Houses, and the well being situated at the foot of a steep hill they kept rowling large ones down from the top of it which were often near doing us much mischief; to prevent this in great measure, it was determined by the officers to set fire to the adjacent Houses which would not only terrifie them but hinder their approaching to molest us, as they then would have no shelter from our muskets. Therefore when the people went onshore again after Dinner, several of them were given post fires for that purpose, when it was amazing with what alacrity they carried this scheme into execution; the eagerness with which they grasped at this small opportunity of revenge being so great that the officers could not keep them in the least order, for they all instantly seprated and were guided only by their own impetuosity setting fire to the Houses and killing the Natives wherever they met with any; who were struck with such terror at seeing the flames that they made off as fast as they could, and it was very fortunate that they did; for our people we so much scattered that had they made the least resistance they might have cut several of them off, and the rest of us known nothing of it till this business was over, which was in about an hour, when with great difficulty we collected the people together and stopped their further progress. During this they had burnt about thirty houses and killed six of the Natives. Two Irishmen concerned in the affair, extended their malice even to the dead bodies, by cutting the heads from two of them, which they brought down and fixed upon the sterns of the boats. While the Houses were yet blazing we perceived a party of them coming down the Hill but upon some of our people firing a few muskets at them they immediately fell flat on the ground and lay still for about five minutes; they then got up and advanced slowly towards us with white flags in their hands, and finding they were not very numerous, we suffered them to approach us – when they proved to be our Friends the priest, whom I mentioned last, with some of his followers coming to entreat for peace for himself and his people. His House being unknown to us, was unfortunately burnt with the others: we carried him onboard the ships where we consoled him in the best manner we could and made him several presents being well convinced of his sincerity to us; when the Natives that came down the Hill perceived the two bodies laying without their heads they set up a most frightfull cry followed with great lamentation seemed to be more affected at that than anything we had done to them, which must arise entirely from superstition.

I cannot proceed without mentioning an instant of remarkable courage in one of these Indians, who had for some time greatly annoyed the waterers, by throwing stones at them from behind the Rocks; at last being closely persued by several of our people he retreated to a deep narrow cave, and immediately began raising a small breastwork of stones towards the bottom of it, behind which he placed himself. They searched all round but to no purpose, and tis a doubt whether they would have found him or not, had not he discovered himself by throwing stones at them the instant they appeared. Upon this three or four of them steped to the entrance of the cave and presented their muskets at him, and at the same time made signs, and told him that if he would come out, he should not be hurt; when like AEneas, he returned an answer with a flying stone, which was followed by others as fast as he could throw them they then fired at him five or six times at which he seemed to be not in the least intimidated still persisting in throwing at them; but preceiving that he was much wounded and resolved to fight to the last moment, one of them rushed in upon him claped a pistol to his heart and instantly dispatched him. On examining him we found he had received no less than four balls, in different parts. He was tall, well made, handsome, young man and had the appearance of a cheif. We took one of the Natives prisoner that was attempting to escape in his canoe, whom we bound hand and foot and put him into a boat that had the head of one of his Countrymen on the stern of it. In the evening the boat returned onboard having got a sufficiency of water to last us to Towi, one of the other Islands where we knew we could get plenty. The officers would not permit the seamen to bring the two heads onto the ship; but obliged them to throw them into the water, alongside.

The prisoner being brought upon the quarter Deck, and set down bound as before every body thronged round him as is usual in such cases; when it is scarce possible to conceive how strongly every sign of fear was imprinted in his countenance he was seized with a most violent trimbling from head to foot. His complexion which was naturally of a light copper, was changed to that of a pale lead colour; and he remained silent, and immoveable. His apprehensions of death in every horrid form, appeared to be so strong, as not to admit of the least ray of hope to his releif, and entirely deprived him of the faculty of speech – by his looks which expressed the most exquisite distress he seem to implore for mercy, in a manner so affecting, that it excited pitty in every breast and all being desirous for it we unbound him. He now thought we were going to put into execution what his fears had suggested; and when we returned him his Canoe and told him that he might go on shore he paid no attention to it, for sometime; imagining we did it only to insult him in his misery, by tantalizing him with what he had too great a dread upon his mind to believe; but when he found we were in earnest, his excess of joy was then as predominant as his fears had been before; and his gratitude which he expressed in the sincerest manner was not disguised under the vail of politeness, but flowed from the heart free and uncorrupted. He had not been long onshore before he came off again, with his canoe loaded with whatever he could procure, as a present to us; for which in return we gave him something of equal value; this he continued to do two or three times a day and became a most faithfull Friend.

On the 19th the Carpenters having finished the mast, after great difficulty it was got in; the hawser we had used for that purpose being so rotten that it stranded in five or six places as we were heaving, and we had no better onboard. On the 20th in the morning a chief[1] that we had not seen before came onboard to negotiate a peace with us; and promised to restore part of the Captains Body. Accordingly in the afternoon Capt Clerke with three of the boats well armed went close inshore on the Southside where he concluded a peace with that cheif; and brought on board Capt Cooks head and hands which were all the remains we could possibly procure. The head was too much disfigured to be known but one of the hands, we were well assured was his from a wound he had formerly received in it which made it remarkable.[2] One of the Natives brought about an handfull of small human bones which he said belonged to the Marines whome they had burnt; we made several enquiries to

1 This man was probably a chief of the Kona district, called Hiapo.
2 Cook had a distinctive scar between the thumb and finger of his right hand.

know if they eat them but could not find the least reason to believe so; for they seemed to express as great an abhorrence of such an act as any European. They told us that no part of Capt Cook was burnt but what became of the remainder of his Body we could not learn[1]; they also brought off the double barreled peice he had with him when he was killed but they had entirely spoiled it by beating the barrels quite flat at the muzzle; we could never get the least intiligence of the cutter that was stolen, which was the first cause of the unfortunate affair.

On the 21st some of the Natives from the Southside of the Bay brought off provisions and began to traid with us as usual; but excepting the old priest we were seldom visited by any of those on the Northside, who did not seem so much inclined as the others .to come to a reconciliation. Yet! from every appearance I make no doubt had we remained there but that in three or four weeks we should have been nearly upon as friendly terms with them as we were at our first coming.

In the afternoon we buried the remains of our much lamented Commander, alongside with every ceremony due to His Rank; whose name will be perpetuated to after ages and ever stand foremost on the list of British Navigators.

On the 22nd the ship being rigged again, and ready for sea in the morning we sailed out of the Bay, having no desire to stay any longer at a place where we had suffered so great a misfortune. And I make no doubt but the principal part of the Natives were much rejoiced at our departure. We stood along shore to the North as we had done before for 10 or 12 Leagues and then bore away from the Island, having now sailed round upwards of ¾ of it without seeing any other harbour or Bay but that we were in.

′ After leaving Owyhee [Hawaii] we stood towards three high Islands, that lie to the Northwards of it, in the parallel of

---

1 It seems very probable that Cook's body was given the ceremonial ritual due to a
   high chief, after which treatment the hair and various bones were distributed to
   several other chiefs, in accordance with Hawaiian custom.

Maw, wee [Maui] and in sight from both; they don't appear to be quite so fertile as the others in the Cluster, and seeing no signs of any harbour we did not stop, but after passing close along the SW side of them we directed our course to the NW for the Island we had first seen in coming from the Southward last year, but we being then too far to leeward, could not fetch it, and was obliged to bear away for another, as is there mentioned.

After two days sail, we made the Island and came to an anchor, in a small open road, on the NE side of it; the interior part is hilly, the shore low and exceeding well cultivated but very bare of wood. The Natives here don't appear to be very numerous and as soon as we came near the land they ventured onboard, without any hesitation and were very friendly; the first enquiry we made was about yams, of which they informed us they had plenty and would bring some off to us the next day. As these, and water, were now our principal objects, the two Captains went onshore to look for the latter, which they found, and in the general opinion of every one else that saw it, was good and to be got at without much difficulty. Altho this place appeared to be in every respect more convenient for our purpose than that we were going to, yet! Capt Clerke did not approve of our staying here, and in the evening sailed from the Island; which is called by the Natives Oowahoo [Oahu]. It lies in Lat: 21½°N and Long: 202° East and is about N W by W 40 Leagues from the three Islands we passed by after leaving Owyhee being much the larger space in the Cluster.

March
1779

Kauai

From hence we stood to the WNW for Towi [Kauai] which is about 25 Leagues distance and the next day came to an anchor in Ohamaya Road; where we had been before in January 1778. We were visited by the Natives as usual, who seemed to be very well pleased at seeing us again and in a short time the ships were surrounded with Canoes; they brought off with them plenty of provisions which we purchased, being very acceptable, as we began to be in want of some. The next morning the Launches and some other boats with a party under

the Command of Mr King our first Lieut were sent onshore.
Having landed they were received by a great number of the
Natives, apparantly in a very friendly manner, who under
pretence of traiding intermixed with them and soon began to be
troublesome by taking and running away with whatever
they could lay hold of; and one of them even became so daring
as to snatch a Bayonet from the side of one of the Marines,
which he got clear off with. Mr King preceiving this judged it too
dangerous to continue on shore any longer with the few people
he had with him, and those not all armed. He therefore gave
over watering and colected them altogether retreated gradually
down to the beach; which they were lucky enough to reach and
put off all safe, tho not without great hazard and difficulty, being
obliged to fire three or four muskets to keep back the Natives
who had followed them close down to the waterside, and
thrown several stones and spears which chanced to do no hurt.
As this was the only place left at these Islands where we could get
water to take with us to the Northward, we were obliged to
attempt it again, at any risk; accordingly in the morning the
launch was sent from each ship with empty casks and a gang of
people for that purpose; likewise four other boats with about 40
men who were cheifly Marines, as a guard for their protection.
They formed onshore in a regular manner, and kept constantly
underarms, by which means tho' the Natives were very
numerous, yet! we kept them at a distance; and very peaceable,
none daring to come near us but such as we chose to permit that
we might traid with them. During this they came off to the ships
which lay about a mile from the shore in great numbers and
brought onboard plenty of provisions of every kind except
yams which we was most in want of, they being very scarce. In
three or four days we compleated our water, which was
exceeding good, without any further disturbance with the
Natives, but finding that we could not procure a supply of yams
here as we expected; after a stay of about a week we sailed for
the Island of Neehow [Nihau] and the same day came to an

anchor in an open road on the leeside of it, where we lay last year.

Our whole employment here was in traiding for yams which we not only purchased along sides from the Natives who were very friendly but had boats onshore every day for that purpose. We enquired concerning two gotes, that we had left with them when we were here before, which I had forgot to mention; and they informed us that after our departure the people of Towi, who are far more powerfull than they in every respect, had demanded them and on their refusing to deliver them up, a battle ensued; wherein they being much worsted by way of putting an end to the dispute had killed the goats rather than the other people should have them.

After useing every method in our power to procure yams, we got only a sufficient quantity to last us three weeks; which was far short of what we wished for, or even expected. But finding that we would get no more, and the spring advancing fast, after a weeks stay here and near four month amongst these Islands, on the 16th of March 1779 we sailed for the Northward to prosecute our Discoveries another season in search of a passage thro' the Ice above Behring straits. As Capt Cook had given the name of Sandwich to these Islands we first discovered it was now continued to the whole Cluster which are nine in number; and extend from 19° to 22° North Lat: and from 199° to 206° East Longitude. Owyhee which is by far the most extensive is of a circular form about 25 Leagues across, and is at least eight times as large as Otaheite it lies exceedingly convenient for the Spanish ships to tutch at in their passage from Acapulca to Manilla; being in the parallel of both and about 980 Leagues distance from the former, and 1600 from the latter: therefore tis very probably that in a few years, they will have a settlement upon it. The interior parts rises into two very high mountains[1], whos summits are covered with eternal

The
Hawaiian
Islands

1 Mauna Kea, 13,825 feet, and the active volcano, Mauna Loa, which figured much in Hawaiian mythology.

snow tho' in so warm a climate the shores appear to be every where fertile except on the Northside which seems entirely burnt up; and bears evident proof of there having been formerly great eruptions from some volcano upon these mountains; but tho' we perceive no smoak arising from them as we have seen in the Coast of America, yet! have reason to believe they still continue in a small degree. Mowwee the easter most Island of the Cluster[1] and the next in extent is 14 or 15 Leagues in extent and 7 or 8 in breadth; Morrohoi, Owahoo and Towi are nearly alike, being circular and about 9 or 10 Leagues across. Kahowruwe, Kanni and Neehow are likewise nearly equal in size to one another being about four Leagues each way. These with a small high Island to the westward of Neehow and in sight from it called Taoora, make up the number.

The productions of these Islands are Bread fruit, sweet potatoes, sugar cane, plantains, bananoes, eddy root, and the Cloth tree; all in greater plenty than we had ever met with before; particularly the sugar cane which was the largest we had ever seen, and is much superior to that in the West Indies. One I recolect that after the head was broke off measured eleven feet in length and eleven inches in circumference. Yams we got only to leeward and Cocoa nuts, that are so very plentifull at all other Islands between the Tropicks, we found only at Carriacoah Bay; and there exceeding scarce. The Soil here is not so rich as at the Society and Friendly Islands but the plantations are perportionally much more numerous and extensive, these Indians being more Industrious and improve in cultivation than any we have seen. The principal part is the Cloth tree, the eddy root, sweet potatoes, and yams; the other productions require little or no labour, but grow almost spontaneously. The quadrupeds here are Hoggs and Dogs; the former very numerous but the latter rather scarce. Whether there are rats or not as at Otaheite I can't determine, but don't

1 The islands he refers to are, in order, Maui, Molokai, Oahu, Kauai, Kahoolawe, Lanai, Niihau, Kaula.

remember ever to have seen any. The few birds they have were small and only remarkable for their plumage, being cheifly of the Paroquet kind as at most of the other Tropical Islands. Indeed! there is one sort that is very small and all its feathers are intirely red, which I don't recolect to have met with at any other place; Fowls are very plentifull here and exactly the same as in England. But we never saw any of their eggs either at these or the Islands to the Southward, which is rather surprising. As I dont know anything else the Natives have got, that they did not bring to sell to us; therefore I suppose they make no use of them, and imagin we would not either, and as we were not in want of them tis probable they was never enquired for. There are very few fish here, and those small and indifferent; yet! the Natives are exceeding fond of them and as often eat them raw as broiled; their only method of fishing, that I know of, is with hook and line at which they are very expert, and assiduous.

As we could have no idea of falling in with these Islands when we were to the Southward we had disposed of all our Cattle there except the two goats mentioned at Neehow, which was very unlucky; for a breed of oxen in particular would have been of much greater use here to future Navigators than either at the Society or Friendly Islands, as Owihee is far more extensive for them to increase upon, and there being plenty of salt to cure them with for sea.

The Natives at these Islands from the lowest computation that can be made of their numbers, are not less than half a million; being far more numerous than at any others yet discovered, between the Tropicks in the Pacific Ocean. Their complexion is a just medium between those of the Friendly and the Society Islands, but in every other respect they resemble the former, having the same robust primitive and warlike appearance; and are entirely free from the Indolent effeminacy so predominate in the latter and altho we had several quarrels with them, they are certainly much more civilized, more generous, and sincere, and possessed of a greater share of understanding than any other Indians we met with during the voyage.

The women here tho' not so fair as in general at the Society Islands, yet! are quite as agreeable, if not more so, their Features are regular and beautiful their mien gracefull, both in their persons and dress neat, their dispossions mild and cheerfull and their whole study and endevour to render themselves pleasing to every one; they seem to be fonder of singing and dancing in their own mode than any Girls we have ever seen; and notwithstanding, there is a great degree of laciviousness in both yet! It is attended with a peculiar kind of simplicity and inocence which joined to the customs of the Country entirely removes every idea that can be formed to their prejudice. In fact so pleasing is their tempers, so great their vivacity, that even an hermit could not help being delighted with them.

The Language spoken at New Zealand, the Friendly, and Society Islands is likewise used here with no great variation tho' at such a distance from each other but it agrees nearest with that of the latter.

The Cloth they make here is not so fine as at Otaheite; nor have they got such quantities of it; yet! it is far preferable as being very strong and equally so whether wet or dry, which must be owing to some difference in the process of manufacturing it that we are not aquainted with, as I don't recolect that any of us ever saw them at that work. Some pieces they paint of three or four different colours and in a great variety of patterns; which appeared very Beautifull and was what we had not seen before. The men wear no more of it than what they do at the other Islands, and the women have only one piece wrapt round their waist, which reaches down to their knees leaving their sholders and breasts entirely bare as at the Friendly Islands.

It is very extroordinary that the hair of those Indians when permitted to grow long naturally forms into seperate locks which are clotted together like the wool of a black sheep, and exactly resemble it, being always of that colour; and faded at the ends in the same manner, to a light brown, by the heat of the sun. The men in general cut it all close off on each side preserving only a range in the middle about two inches broad reaching from the forehead down to the neck; which they dont suffer to grow above two inches long, and either curls or stands upright. The women also have theirs all cut off very short except a small quantity along the fore part of their heads which lies flat upon the crown and is about fives inches long withe the ends faded as before mentioned; this fashion at first appeared very drole, but custom soon reconsiled it to us, and we began to think it looked tolorable well, but not equal to the long flowing locks of the Girls of Otaheite.

Tattowing seems not to be so much practiced here by either sex, as at the Islands to the southward, and the custom of the women not being alowed to eat in the presence of the men which is there so strictly observed is taken no notice of here. The first time we lay at Carriacoah Bay some of our Gentlemen formed into parties of three of four together and went up into the Country for a few days taking one or two Indians with them as Guides and attendants. They found the Island neither inhabited nor cultivated beyond six or seven miles from the shore; where it began to be very woody and continued so for a considerable height up the mountains. The ground seemed to be hollow underneath them, in several places from the resounding of their footsteps as they walked along; and they discovered here and there small channels of dryed Lava with other convincing proofs of former eruptions. They were never in the least molested by the Natives but on the contrary always met with great hospitality and were suffered to go where ever they pleased. I had forgot to mention before that one evening while we were there we displayed the remainder of our fireworks onshore in the presence of a numerous assembly collected upon this occasion, who were all greatly surprized, and delighted with them, particularly with the sky rockets which seemed to excite their admiration more than any of the others.

The yava root is more plentifull here than at the Islands to the Southward and is used by the cheifs to a great excess. The method of prepairing it is exactly the same as has been discribed.

The whole of their cookery consists in baking, roasting and broiling, being intirely unaquainted with boiling from having no kind of vessel that will bear the fire for heating water.

The Chiefs here wear on particular occasions a cap of fine wicker work which is very neatly made; and has a very narrow ridge along the middle of it about two inches high, exactly resembling an ancient Helmet; and in the same manner as they have their own Hair; the out side is entirely covered with feathers put on in stripes of four different colours, viz: red, yellow, green and black, which looks very beautifull and war like; they also wear with it a cloak of fine netting covered with feathers of the same colours formed into regular squares within one another appearing very elegunt.

Owyhee is the only one of these Islands that we have any knowledge of relative to its Government which seems to be much like that at Tongataboo the largest of the Friendly Islands. From what we can learn the Regency is hereditary and the King altho he has great power and is shewn every kind of respect, yet! is far from being absolute of himself; but with the joint consent and assistance of the cheifs is very much so, by whom those people are kept under more subjection than any we have seen. They are exceeding superstitious and the priests seem to have great authority over them; but the principles of their Religion I'm quite unacquainted with. We saw several kinds of Images about their Houses and burying places, but what they esteem most are a sort of household God in the Figure of a mans head; which are of slite wicker work and entirely covered with small red feathers. The eyes are represented by two pieces of mother of pearl shell and the opening of the mouth is furnished with two rows of Hog's teeth; indeed; not only the features but the whole face is distorted in such a drole and rediculous manner, that even the Natives could scarce refrain at times from laughing at them. After much perswasion they were prevailed upon to sell some to us; which was very readily purchased, as being a great curiosity. The only articles we made use of here for traiding was Iron, which they are exceeding fond of in any shape; and seemed to care very little about anything else. They are the only Indians we met with that ever attempted to work it themselves into different forms agreeable to their own fancy; which from seeing our armorers onboard they accomplished neater than could possibly be imagined by heating and beating it with a stone. The Houses here are more collected and formed into Towns and Villages, than at the Southern Island, being there very much scattered. They are rather small, and exactly represent a farmers Barn; the roof is thatched as at the other Islands, but they differ in being enclosed all round, except a space for a door at one end and a small hole on each side to admit the light. The inside is always kept neat and clean having generally mats spread all over it.

The Small single Canoes here are nearly like those at the Friendly Islands with outriggers to them, in the same manner, and both in their form and workmanship are the neatest we have ever seen. Their double ones are some what larger than the others which are fixt parallel at about four feet distance, by three of four spars extending (with a curve upwards) from one to the other and lashed down across both; along the middle of those spars they had one or two planks placed, upon which they carry their Hogs, Fruit and what ever they bring off to us; the sailing Canoes are in respect to their sails, masts and riggings much like those at the Society Islands, being very ill contrived, and seemingly as indifferently navigated. They dont appear to have any here particularly adapted for War as we found at Oteheite.

Several of those Indians who have not got Canoes have a method of swimming upon a piece of wood nearly in the form of a blade of an oar; which is about six feet in length, sixteen inches in breadth at one end and about 9 at the other; and is four or five inches thick, in the middle, tapering down to an inch at the sides. They lay themselves upon it length ways, with their breast about the centre; and it being sufficient to buoy them up they paddle along with their hands and feet at a modrate rate, having the broad end foremost; and that it may not meet with any resistance from the water, they keep it just above the surface by weighing down upon the other, which they have underneath them, between their legs. These pieces of wood are so nicely balanced that the most expert of our people at swimming could not keep upon them half a minuit without rolling off.

The Cheif employments carried on by these people are cultivation, fishing, the manufacturing of their cloth, and building their Houses and Canoes; but none of them are laborious except the latter which is very much so. The wood they use for that purpose is rather hard and in general two or three miles from the shore; and there being no metal here the principle mechanical tool they have to fell the trees with, and then to cut them into plank, is a stone hatchet which renders both very tedious and it is surprising how they manage to make such a number of canoes as they have got under the circumstances.

I had forgot to observe before that during our stay at these Islands we did not use an article of the ships provisions, but subsisted entirely upon what we purchased; which was another great help to our sea stock, and refreshed us very much. Likewise that we salted as much pork as almost lasted us to England, which kept exceeding well, all the time.

We sailed from hence with great dissatisfaction, on account of the Death of our unfortunate Commander which still lay heavy upon our minds, as being truly sensible of our loss; this together with the thoughts of the approching season to the North. The hardships of the last being still recent in our memory – and will never be effaced from mine – rendered us quite dispirited.

Chapter Five

KAMCHATKA

From these Islands we directed our course to the Westward keeping in the traid winds till we came to the meridian of Kamchatka, and then hauled up to the Northwards.

About a fortnight after leaving the land, we met with a very hard gale of wind which caused the ship to spring a leak; on the starboard bow we did not perceive it before the hatch that covers the passage into the coal hole was burst open from the place being full of water. We instantly scuttled the bulk heads forewards to bring it to the pumps, with which and constant bailing with buckets for two or three days, we kept it under, and the gale fortunately then abated, and the leak ceased. During this we were greatly alarmed at our situation; as being at least three weeks sail from the nearest land; and even that was the coast of Japan where we could not hope for the smallest assistance, but might rather expect to be cut off or made slaves by those people. April 1779

After a passage of about six weeks, on the 26th of April 1779 we made the Eastern coast of Kamchatka; in Latitude 52°N the land in general is very high and covered with snow, presenting a most dreary and uncomfortable prospect; we at this time experienced a greater severity of cold, than ever we had done before, every part of the ship being covered in Ice and Snow. We turned up to the Northward till the 30th when we came to an anchor in the entrance of the Bay of Awatcha which was our intended port. The next morning we weighed and stood into it; and in the evening anchored within about two miles of the Ostrog, or village of St. Peter and St. Paul, not being able to get any further for a firm body of Ice which extended that distance from the shore. A day or two before we came in the Discovery by some means parted Company, and mistaking the entrance into the Bay did not put in till three days after us; this was the only time the two Ships were seprated during the voyage.[1]

Avacha Bay

This Bay is situated on the east Coast of Kamchatka in Lat: 53°N and Long: 158° 50′ East. The entrance is bold to on each side and about ½ a mile wide for about a mile and an half up; from whence it opens into nearly a circular form, about three Leagues across. It receives its name from the River Awatcha which empties it self at the bottom of it, as does also a smaller River called Paratoonka from an ostrog about three miles up it; the former is large and navigatable for boats a great distance up, but the latter not much higher than the Ostrog.

Within this Bay there are three excellent Harbours; two of them are very deep and commodious, but the other off which we lay, is rather small; it is circular and about half a mile over and formed by a long and narrow neck of land upon which is the Ostrog of St. Peter and St. Pauls, from whence it is named. There is a modrate and regular tide here, with good anchorage from 10 to 20 fathoms both in the entrance and all over the Bay, except at the bottom of it; where it is shoal for two miles. That part of the shore between the two Rivers is low and marshy for some distance but every way else is very hilly and terminates in steep Cliffs, craggy points and large sandy beaches; very convenient for hauling the seine for fish which are exceeding plentifull here. There are several small Lagoons of fresh water full of Trout; and scarce a valley without large rivulets running

1 This is not true; they were separated for some days off the Hawaiian coast in January, 1778, and, of-course, on the journey from England to Capetown.

through it and falling into the Bay. On the southside of the
entrance there is a very high mountain and two close together to
the NE further inland from the coast; one of these is a volcano,
as is that to the Southwards; the country is tolerably well
wooded with birch which is the only kind that grows here. At
present we found it entirely covered with snow and the shore
surrounded with Ice by which the Harbour was quite blocked
up. We were greatly deceived in the appearance of the Ostrog
of St. Peter and St. Paul, for from the account given us of it at
Shamganooda we expected to find a large populous Town; but
on the contrary it consists only of six wretched log houses and 8
or 10 Kamseadale ones;[1] and instead of a Fort, with forty Guns,
as we had been informed they have only two pieces of small
cannon here, one of them a 3 pounder and the other a one
pounder, mounted upon a couple of ill made carriages without
any kind of fortification what ever. There are not above thirty
five Rusians, and they are all soldiers under the command of a
Sergeant, who is the principle person at this place; The
Kamseadales likewise dont appear to be numerous.

   They were very much alarmed at our appearence in the Bay;
and the forenoon after we came in, when Mr King our Lieut and
some other Gentlemen went to the Ostrog, they found them all
under arms each having a large riffled barrled musket ready to
act with on the defensive if occasion required. Our gentlemen
were very politely received by the Sergeant who showed them
every civility in his power and conducted them to his house,
where he prepared a dinner for them in the best manner he
could which consisted principally on fish and rye bread with it.
He would not by any means be prevailed upon to sit down but
stood and waited upon them himself. They had never seen any
ships before, and had no idea who we were or from whence we
came, appearing to have no knowledge of the states of Europe;
and very unluckily we had no person onboard that could speak

1 The Kamseadale people Gilbert saw here (Kamchatkans) were in residence as
   servants in the Russian settlement.

the Rusian Language, so that we were not able to satisfy them in these points, or yet to tell them what our business was there – whether our intentions were friendly or hostile, for they seemed to be greatly in fear of the latter. It now plainly appears that the account given us of this place by the Captain of the Rusian vessel at Shamganooda Harbour was mearly to intimidate us and if possible to prevent our going there, as he fancied we might have a design against it. Mr King delivered the two letters we had received from him to the Sergeant; one being for himself and the other for the Governor of Kamchatka which was immediately sent express to Bolchoireeka,[1] the Capital Town of the Country, where he resided.

May
1779About a week afterwards two people arrived here from thence one of them a kind of Merchant, and the other an attendant upon the Governor, who very fortunately was a German. As Mr Webber our painter understood that Language tollerably well, some of our officers waited upon them at the Ostrog, and were informed by the German that they was sent by the Governor to learn who we were, and likewise our intentions; for the letter they received, had put them into great consternation as the Rusian Capt at Shamganooda had expressed in his opinion that we were pirates and had a design against the Country; and the Governor having no Intelligence of our being in these parts, was at a great loss how to account for us, or what to do upon the occasion. We fully explained ourselves to them thro Mr Webber, and removed every doubt to their entire satisfaction; and they now shewed us that civility with pleasure which before they had done thro' fear and came onboard the ships where we entertained them in the best manner we could. The Sergeant likewise now ventured onboard, which he had not done before tho' we often invited Him.

After a stay of about two days, Capt Gore, Mr King and Mr Webber, with two servants set out with them for Bolchorreeka,

1 Bolsheretsk, on the other side of the peninsula, the government and trade centre.

to pay their respects to the Governor, and make known to him our business and situation; he received them with the greatest pleasure, and politeness imaginable, and was happily relieved from the fear and perplexity that our arrival had occasioned amongst them.[1] He was a Major in the Rusian Service and had the Government of the whole Country; and very luckily too was a German, which saved the trouble of any other interpreter as Mr Webber was present.

The Ostrog or Town of Bolchorreeka is situated on the west coast of Kamchatka in Lat: 52° 54′ North and Long: 156° 37′ East. It consists of about 100 Houses and 400 Inhabitants of whom 150 are Rusian soldiers, and the rest trading people and Kamseadales. I believe they have got five or six pieces of Cannon here but no garrison or any kind of fortification in the whole Country. The Major whose name was Behm, gave our officers the best entertainment the place could afford and made them several valuable presents, consisting cheifly of very rich furs made into Cloaks and Caps. After they had been there two or three days he set out with them for Awatcha Bay to see the ships, where he arrived after a very tedious journey of a week, tho' it is not above 80 miles, which was occasioned by the Frost then breaking up and the snow going away.

The next day having put the ships in order for his reception, a boat with an officer was sent to the Ostrog, to bring Him onboard. On his coming we saluted Him with 15 Guns, and received Him with a guard of Marines, and every respect due to His Rank. He dined with Capt Clerke who shew Him every civility in His power and in the evening returned ashore again; the next day he dined onboard the Discovery with Capt Gore and afterwards with the officers of the Resolution. He seemed to be highly delighted with the entertainment He met with, as we made use of every effort in our power to make it agreeable to Him. He stayed here five or six days, and then returned home;

---

1 The governor was a generous and helpful man named Magnus von Behm, who helped supply the ships at his own expense.

having procured us what little supply the place could afford at
present and promised to send round from Bolchorreeka every
thing they could possibly spare to be ready for us at our return
from the Northwards. As he intended this Summer to resign His
Government, and return to Rusia, we took that oppertunity to
send Dispatches to England.[1]

After we had been here about a fortnight the Ice between us
and the shore broke loose and drifted out of the Bay; we then
warped within half a mile of the Ostrog, and moored with the
Bowers a cable each way. We did not go into the Harbour this
Time, as it was not clear of Ice till the latter end of May. We set
up our observatories as usual ashore at the Ostrog, for the
purpose of making astronomical observations. Our time keeper
very unfortunately by some accident got spoiled, and we had no
person onboard that understood how to repair it; but that
belonging to the Discovery continued to keep very good time
all the voyage. We took in a great quantity of wood and water
here both being very plentifull and easy to be got at, in every
part of the Bay. Our casks, sails and rigging, we overhauled and
repaired in the best manner we could, all of them being now
very much worn and become exceeding bad; and we had but
little canvas, or cordage remaining in stores, and the latter
nearly dry rotten.

The only refreshments the Country afforded at this time were
Cod, Herrings and Trout, which, latterly we caught in great
quantities; the Former with hook and line along side, and the
others with the seine. As soon as the Beaches was clear of Ice
and snow which was not till the middle of May. The only
vegitable we found here, was garlick; which springs up every
where very plentifully as soon as the snow is off the ground.

The Houses belonging to the Rusians are small and have a
very wretched appearance; they are built with long straight logs
of wood laid horizontally one upon the other, each having a

1 This was how the news of Cook's death reached the Admiralty, and then the
European public, seven months later.

small grove on the upper part, along which they lay some dryed
moss to keep out the cold before they place the next log upon it.
They are roofed and thatched in the manner of a Farmers barn
and are generally divided into two rooms, with one or two
windows in each made of Talc instead of glass, as they have not
got any at this place. They are so very close and warm within as
in the midst of winter to have but little occasion for fire. Their
bed places are built, up along the sides, and covered with bear
skins, serving them also for seats in the day time. The inside of
these Houses are generally remarkable dirty throughout but
that they seemed to be not the least concerned about, being
themselves in point of cleanliness very little better than the
Indians at King Georges Sound.

Their common dress resembles the European except in
having fur Jackets, and Caps, which soon have a very filthy
appearance as they never take the trouble to clean them; they
are likewise equally dirty in their persons for I don't think that
they wash or shave themselves above once a fortnight.

They are all drawn up under Arms every morning and evening
and reviewed by the sergeant, and keep two or three sentinels in
different parts of the Ostrog day and night. On these occasions
they put on their Regimental Coat, which is green faced with red
and very little cleanlier than their other dress. The officers that
afterwards came here except two or three of the highest Rank
were likewise in every respect exceeding slovenly. The only
Rusian women in this Country were the wives of Major Behm
and Capt Smiloff.[1] The houses belonging to the Kamseadales are
called Ballangans and are placed in the middle of a square
platform eight or ten feet from the ground supported by a number
of upright posts, and made of spars laid athwart from one to
the other, which are covered with small branches, reeds and
dryed grass sufficient for them to walk upon and to keep the
rain from going through, for under it they dry their fish. On one
side there is a ladder fixed that they ascend by to their house,

1 Captain Schmalov, deputy governor of Kamchatka.

which is small and does not take up above half of the platform. It consists of several spars placed in a circular manner at the bottom and meeting in a point at the top in the form of a cone; and is surrounded with reeds and straw except a small space to enter at but scarcely sufficient to exclude the cold and rains. The Kamseadales appear to be kept in a state of very strict subjection to the Rusians, they differ but little from the Natives at Shamganooda Harbour on the oposite part of the Coast of America; being like them short in stature, with flat faces and nearly the same likeness in their features, but of a fairer complexion. They seem to be of a very quiet and mild disposition and seldom speak but when real occasion requires. The dress cheifly consists of furs and skins, made into Caps and Jackets, in which they are more cleanly than the Rusian soldiers. The women are in general tolerable decent in their dress, being much more so than the men; especially those that are married to the Rusians, who are habited nearly in the European Fashion. They have a round flat face with small features, and a very fair complexion, their disposition is exceeding mild but quite devoid of all kind of mirth and vivacity, being very different in that respect from the Ladies of the Tropical Islands; yet! there is something innocent and pleasing in their Countenances which much resembles that of the Chinese, between whom and the esqimaux Indians at Hudsons Bay, these people may be looked upon as a just medium.

The winter in this Country begins about the latter end of November and continues till the middle of May. The ground all that time being covered with snow and the Frost very severe, during that interval the cheif sustenence of these people is dryed salmon and rye bread, and flower, which is the only grain they have and is very course and even of that they are put to a certain allowance, on account of scarcity, as it does not grow here but is brought from Ochoz [Okhotsk] a large Town on the adjacent coast of Siberia, 200 Leagues to the NW of

Bolchoireeka. A small vessel comes from thence round the south point of Kamchatka every Summer with that principally, and other supplies for this place. On our arrival we found several of the Rusians very much afflicted with the scurvey, which is always the case about that time; and we were informed that frequently some of them die of it, before the return of the Spring. It's cheifly brought on by their unparaleled indolence, for during the whole winter they very seldom stir out of their Houses, or use any kind of exercise; but oblige the Kamseadales to do all their work and get them whatever they want. As this keeps the latter employed, it is the reason of their being so much more healthy than the Rusians, who would all be carried off by this disorder was it not for the great quantities of garlick they eat as soon as it springs up; which is the only vegetable they make use of. For tho these settlements have been made upwards of 80 years, yet they have no kind of European vegitation here or a single foot of ground cultivated, except a small spot we afterwards found with a few turnips on it, which are scarce worth mentioning, as I dont recolect seeing a dozen of them.

There was a small one masted sloop frozen up in the Harbour which was to sail for Ochoz in the Summer; she was about sixty or eighty tons Burthen remarkably ill built, being far more clumsey than a Dutch Dogger. They have only got five or six sail of small vessels in these parts and one of them goes every other Summer to their settlements, upon the Islands off the Coast of America near the Neck of Alaska where we met with them. She is sent out with Rye, Flower, ammunition and other necessaries for the support of the people there; and returns with furs of which they procure great quantity along that Coast. This passage tho not above 400 Leagues generally takes them six or eight weeks to perform it, these vessels being extraordinary dull Sailors, and the Rusians as inexpert Navigators. At the head of the Harbour there is a storehouse, and an hospital, built with logs by Capt Behring before he set out on his expidition to the Coast of America.

The method of travelling here, in the winter over the Ice is in sledges very neatly constructed: the lower part is two flat pieces of light wood five or six inches broad, and seven or eight feet long, rising in a small curve at each end and placed parallel at about sixteen inches distance; upon them they have a seat fixed about a foot and a half high, and so contrived as to be convenient either for sitting or sleeping in. It is 16 or 18 inches broad and five or six feet long, rising 6 or 8 inches on each side and at the ends, in a curve upwards a foot; having just room enough for one person to lie down in, the frame of the seat is slight wood which is closed round with thongs of seahorse hide; and the whole sledge is so light that it may be lifted with one hand with great ease. To this carriage they harness either four or six large dogs, which draw in pairs being very strong and of the wolf kind; for they never bark but always howl like that animal and are exceeding fierce and numerous. The people here esteem them as much as the Europeans do horses, and always choose the largest to train up while they are young to the sledge, which after great trouble in the management of them they will draw very steady and at the rate of five or six miles an hour for that time only; but with stopping a little now and then to rest, they will continue to go three or four miles an hour for an whole day. When once brought up to this, they are ever afterwards tied up in kennel, and not permitted to run loose among the others.

The quadrupeds native to this Country are the wild Deer, which is very scarce, the Black Bear, dog, fox, racoon, martin, and beaver. The Rusians have a few oxen here but we procured only five, which was drove hither from a neighbouring ostrog on purpose for us, being all they could possibly spare at that time; as for sheep, goats, and hogs, they are not possessed of nor yet any kind of poultry; we saw two or three horses but they are very rare.

The first object and support of these settlements are furs, the principle part of which they get from the adjacent coast of

America as this Country is nearly drained of that commodity; for they now procure only the established Tribute from the Natives who bring none to sell as they did formerly. They carry on a small trade by land to the North of China with some of them, but the greatest part is sent to Rusia, from whence they get all their necessaries.

Two merchants as they are there called, but may more properly be termed pedlers, came over from Bolchoireeka to Awatcha Bay on account of our being there, with several sorts of good for sail: viz: Linin, plain and checkered, yarn, stockings handkerchiefs, caps, shoes, boots; a few Chinese silks, with buckles, spoons, knives &c.; which were all exceeding dear, and of the worst quality. The three last articles, and every-thing of the hardware kind were made in England for exportation; we purchased of them a small quantity of tea and sugar which they got from China and they were very eager to trafick with us for the Furs we got on the Coast of America, which were but few, having then very little of any thing left to procure them with from the Indians. For those we sold here we received from 25 to 35 Rublees for each skin which is from £5.6s to £7.9s, a Rublee being reckoned at 4s.3d Sterling. The Kamseadales are mostly employed in fowling and fishing, being very expert in both but the Rusians are in general too lazy to attend to either. Wild ducks and geese are very plentifull upon the low ground between the Rivers and afford excellent shooting.

Their boats here are flat bottomed, broad in the middle and taper to a point at each end being very ill made; their nets likewise are indifferent and in the form of our seine. There is neither wine nor spirituous liquors of any kind in this Country. Yet! both the Rusians and Kamseadales are so exceeding fond of Brandy or Rum that they would give us from four to six Rublees for a quart bottle full, which they never diluted with water but always drank it in drams untill they became quite intoxicated; indeed the latter would not leave off so long as they had the least use of their senses remaining.

        We were supplied here with what little Rye Flower they could spare at present; which tho extreemly bad, yet, was very acceptable in our situation, for by this addition to that we had taken in at the Cape of Good Hope still remaining, we were enabled to be at full allowance of that article in lieu of Bread all the second Season to the Northward. Altho this would not last out the day so well nor was by any means so desirable as the same weight in Biscuit, yet it was far preferable to two thirds allowance, which we must otherwise have continued at, for at these times the quantity of our provisions was a much greater object to us than the quality.

The settlements at this Bay appear rather to be in a state of decay than of improvement, for the Rusians don't seem to make any effort either to extend their Navigation, or increase the number of their vessels. And so great is their indolence that they rather choose to live in the most wretched state of any people we ever saw, than to be at the least labour to cultivate the Country: which from the appearance we afterwards found it to have at our return in from the Northwards is exceeding fertile and would produce any or all of the plants, and roots we have in our gardens, in nearly as great perfection, for tho' the Summer does not continue above four or five months, yet! the ground is no sooner clear of snow but what vegitation there is here, springs up with amazing rapidity, and ripen in like manner. From the appearance of this place at any time of the year, it is throughout in such a perfect state of nature, that was it viewed by a person who did not know what Country it was, nothing else except chancing to see some of the Rusian soldiers in their Regimentals could induce him to imagine that any Europeans inhabited it.

At Parratoonka, a small ostrog, about 12 miles from where we lay, they have a church, which is the only one in this part of the Country. It is built with logs in the manner of their Houses but is much larger; the outside has a very mean appearence, but they have been at great labour to decorate it within, being far

more neat and elegant than could be expected from the
wretched state of every thing else. The alter is enclosed with
painted rails about three feet high and very neat green curtains
hanging over them which draw up and let down at pleasure; the
Table within is covered with a green cloth surrounded with a
deep embroidary of Gold. Over it upon the wall are placed
three large paintings: the extreme one of our Savour and the
Virgin Mary, and that in the middle is a very good one of the
Crucifix, which they pay great respect to, and have a curtain
drawn before it. The pulpit likewise is encircled about with
green hangings and has a crimson Cloth spread over the
forepart with a narrow gold fringe round it. The cushions are
likewise of the same colour with a gold tassel at the outer
corners; between the alter and the pulpit, there is a large and
elegant lamp pendent from the roof. The walls are almost
covered with not less than fifty portraits as large as the life, of
the twelve Apostles, Saints etc. which were all brought hither
from Rusia at a great expence; and are tolerably well executed,
but begin to be very much defaced. They have three small bells
here fixed upon a kind of Gallows a few yards from the Church.
The Priest who is a Native of Rusia is the most intelligent, and
hospitable person that resides near this Bay, and lives in a
much more decent manner. The Religion they profess here, is
that of the Church of Greece.

We were visited by a Rusian Nobleman[1] who had been
upwards of 30 years an exile in this Country; he was now near
60 years of age, and the marks are very visible where his
Nostrils had been slit, which is a customary stamp of disgrace
inflicted upon them before they are sent away. He was greatly
respected here by everyone, and had some time past made
Interest to get the Rank of Proppaschah confered upon him
which is the same of that of an Ensign in our service; but could

1 P. M. Ivashkin, supposed to have been involved in a conspiracy against the life of
   Empress Elizabeth. They actually met this man not on this occasion, but on their
   return to Kamchatka the following September.

not by any means get recalled. However custom had now rendered his banishment so familiar to him, that he had very little desire to return at his time of life. A few years ago a Polish General[1], that had been taken prisoner by the Rusians, was sent here and kept closely confined at Bolchoireeka. He had not been long in that state before he found means to stir up the Kamseadales to an Insurrection, who were soon quelled, but entirely answered his intention in giving him an opportunity to escape; which he effected, and got safe to China from whence they were informed that he went to France. When we arrived here they imagined that he might be returned to harass, and plunder, the Country; as being so well acquainted with their defenceless situation which was chiefly the cause of their great consternation we found them in. Kamchatka is a long neck of land projecting to the southward from the eastern part of Siberia; and extends from 50° to 61½° North Latitude and from 154½° to 163½° East Longitude. Its length is 690 miles and mean breadth about 145 being a little larger than Great Britain, and is 3850 miles distant from Petersburg – it is all in the possession of the Rusians who have not got above five or six Towns of any note in the whole Country, the rest being small Kamseadales Ostrogs, and those not very numerous. The number of Inhabitants here I suppose to be about six or seven hundred of the Former, and four or five thousand of the latter. Tho I have always called these people Rusians, yet! there is scarce one out of ten that really is so; being in general Cossocks, who are soldiers in their service.

Having fitted the ships in the best manner we could and got what little refreshments the place afforded at present; after a stay of near six weeks we weighed but with very great difficulty, being obliged to wait for the flow of the tide which is not above five feet at any time; a twelve fold[2] purchase of a hawser upon

1 M. A. Benyowski, 1771.
2 In this place is inserted Gilbert's only apparent later correction to his narrative. It says: 'Doubtfull a mistake'.

the cable proved ineffectual to bring up the anchor, it being the best holding ground we ever met with. We had no sooner got into the entrance of the Bay but were obliged to come to an anchor; the wind shifted to the Eastward, directly against us.

The next morning was almost calm, at daylight we found our decks covered with fine sand of a light brown colour; which we preceived came from a volcano[1] about 12 Leagues distant from whence a violent eruption had begun in the night and still continued. We very plainly heard an incessant Rumbling noise from it, but could not see the top of the mountain; as it was quite hid in a thick black cloud of smoak, and dust stretching a great way to the NE – by 10 o'clock the dust was at least one fifth of an inch thick upon the decks; and we had then a shower of small stones that lasted a quarter of an hour. Some of them about the size of a pea and others of a horse bean; they were very lite and brittle and of the same colour as the sand, several appearing to have been burnt. During the day we had two more of these showers that did not last above 10 minuits, likewise two or three of rain, which from the atmosphere being so full of Dust the drops in passing thro it were formed into little lumps of mud; we went onshore opposite to the ships but did not preceive the ground trimble or any other signs of an Earthquake. In the evening the eruption began to abate and the next morning was nearly over; the wind then coming fair we weighed and stood out of the Bay which was on the 10th of June 1779.[2]

From hence we stood along shore to the Northward, but did not keep sight of the land above fifteen Leagues before a thick fogg coming on obliged us to haul off from it. In two or three days time the weather cleared up; we stood in again, for the Land, and made it on 54½°N, but had not treaced it above 25 Leagues before we hauld off for a thick fog which made it too

1 Avachinskaya.
2 Actually June 13. His dating is a little erratic here, but they passed through Bering Strait on July 6, and 'fell in with the Ice' the next day.

dangerous to continue our course along shore. After some days having clear weather again we stood in for the Coast and fell in with it once more, in the Lat: 60°N and Long: 166½°E from whence we traced it in an E by N direction for the distance of about 45 Leagues, to the Long: 177° East where it turns off to the North forming a Cape called by the Rusians Tigonooskoi.

July
1779 The weather there coming on very foggy intirely frustrated our intentions of surveying this part of the Coast of Kamchatka and up as high as the straits, a few Leagues to the Southward of which we left last year – what little we saw of it corresponded with the Rusians survey, which were in general very correct, and principally made by that enterprizing Navigator Capt. Behring in the year 1728. The fog still continuing, by the assistance of the Time keeper we passed thro the straits without seeing either continent or the two small Islands in the middle, tho the passage on each side is not above six Leagues wide; which is a convincing proof how much it is to be depended upon. About the latter end of June we fell in with the Ice in Lat: 69°N and then stood to the Eastward to the coast of America, passing thro great numbers of large pieces that had broke loose from the Firm Body, which we traced till we got within 12 or 15 Leagues of the Land; but did not see it, having very foggy and blowing weather. As the Ice prevented our approaching any nearer to this coast, we stood back to the Westward for that of Asia; which we could not reach within 20 Leagues, for the Drift Ice that there extends near two Leagues to the southward of the Main Body. We often got embayed amongst it and could scarce find our way out again; the Discovery was once blocked up for twenty four hours, till a lucky change of wind drove the Ice clear of Her. We killed a few Sea Horses cheifly for their blubber, to melt into oil; but eat very little of them, not being at quite so short allowance as we were the other Season.

The
Arctic
Sea The Drift Ice, was in greater quantities and stritch much further to the southward than it did last Summer; and the firm

Body now extended from shore to shore without any opening in the middle of the sea as there was before, or the least prospect of there being one this year. About the 26th of July after great difficulty and both ships receiving considerable damages we got clear of the Ice; and thinking it unnecessary to continue any longer in search of a passage that nature had then, and I believe, has forever shut against us.[1] We therefore quited the attempt and stood back to the southward for Behring Straits; which we passed through on the 5th of August.

We were becalmed for three or four days off the NW part of a large Island,[2] two degrees to the southward of it. We discovered the east end of this Island last Summer, after leaving Nortons Sound but the weather then being there very bad and foggy we could not determine its extent; we gave it the name of Anderson but I understand that it is since changed to that of our present Commander; its length from east to west is 29 Leagues and breadth twelve Leagues. It is throughout of a modrate height, yet the tops of the hills were still covered with snow; we did not preceive any inhabitants upon it, and the Rusians have not extended their settlements so far to the Northward.

August 1779

After passing by the Western extremity of the Island, our intention was to explore the Coast down to the Bay of Awatcha, but having a continual fogg, all the passage we were again prevented, for that shore being very irregular, it was thought most prudent not to venture near it. We passed within sight of Behring's Islands which are two small ones laying in Lat: 54½° North Long: 168° East, where he was cast away, and died, in the year 1741.

On the 23rd of August[3] we lost our Commander, Capt Clerke, who died of a decline having been ill the greatest part of the voyage. The next day we arrived at the Bay of Awatcha, and

1 On July 19 they reached their most Northerly point for that season, 70° 33'.
2 St. Lawrence Island.
3 Actually August 22, the day after the Kamchatkan coast came in sight again.

there ended the second season to the Northwards, in which we were very unfortunate having had blowing weather and a thick fog, nearly the whole time; so that we could neither make discoveries nor carry on any surveys.

The ships this time went into the Harbour of St Peter and St Pauls, which from its form and security may with great propriety be called a Basin; the entrance is not above a stones throw either in length or breadth and is bold to on each side. Having six fathom water, the soundings within are likewise six and seven fathoms shoaling near the shores to four and three, at the upper part to two fathoms. There are two or three rivulets of excellent water here and very good beaches for hauling the seine. The rise and fall of the tide at full and change is not above five or six feet perpendicular.

Avacha Bay

Captain Gore now took the Command of the Resolution and appointed Mr King our first Lieut to that of the Discovery – whom I followed into that Ship: and Mr William Lanyon one of the Mates was made Lieut: in His Room. The next day we Buried the remains of Capt Clerke onshore a little above the head of the Harbour with the Honors due to His Rank. The appearence of the country was very diffarant at this time of the Year to what it was when we was here before, for instead of Snow the shore was now ever spread with a most delightfull verdure; and altho' every thing was in its rude natural state void of cultivation, there being no Parks, gardens, cornfields; or enclosures, but only Birch trees, Bushes and weeds of various sorts grown up to a great height; yet! to us just come from the Ice they afforded a very pleasing prospect, and the most agreeable Fragrancy I ever met with, which even extended to the ships.

We found some wild raspberries which were equal in flavour to those in England, but very scarce and then almost out of season. Several of the Bushes were full of small red berries of a different kind to any we had seen before; they were not very agreeable to the taste being rather to sower but yielded a great quantity of juice when boiled; in which the Rusians have a method of preserving of them for the winter, yet are in general too indolent to put it inpractice notwithstanding how usefull they would be as a means of securing them against the Scurvy. Hurtle and Cranberries were very plentifull in the vallies; likewise the same kind of herb as we found at Norton Sound, of which we gathered great quantities to use in lieu of Tea, for that we brought out with us being long since expended.

The Discovery since she got blocked up by the Ice had continued to make six or seven inches of water in an hour, from a leak on the starboard bow; we heeled her to starboard, and on examining it found about two feet of the end of a plank close below the wale, stove right in, which luckily had not fallen out afterwards, as it might have occasioned the loss of the ship. This was not the only stroke she received for the other bow was very much damaged; the carpenters of both ships immediately set about repairing them which they compleated in eight or ten days. The Resolution likewise lost great part of her cutwater, and was obliged to be lightened Forwards and hauled with her head upon the Beach at high water to have it repaired; which was done in a few days, and then she hove off again. Our other employment at this place were in carrying on the usual duties such as wooding, watering, repairing sails, rigging etc. and in fishing, for we lived all the time cheifly upon salmon; which were so plentifull at first, that we used to get from forty to sixty, and sometimes near an hundred, at one haul of the seine; but laterly they became more scarce.

The Kamseadales are employed the greater part of the Summer in drying a sufficient quantity of them for their winter support. Each ship salted about ten puncheons to carry to sea with us which proved of very little use, for as we were going to the southward, when we came into warm weather they all spoiled. One of the seamen belonging to the Resolution died here being the first person we lost by sickness since leaving

September 1779

England.[1] The sloop that was laying in the Harbour when we went to the Northward had sailed for Ochoz. We were visited by Captain Smiloff, who now had the Government of the whole Country, to whom we showed every respect in our powers. He staid with us eight or ten days and then returned to Bolchoireeka.

A galiot of 100 or 120 Tons, and very clumsily built, arrived here from thence with stores and provisions and about 50 soldiers who were going to a Town to the Northwards; they had been two month on the passage and were now very sickly. Major Behm accoarding to his promise, sent round in her such things as had been mentioned to him, and as much of each article as they could possibly spare, which were very acceptable to us and much more than we had reason to expect from the state of the Country. This welcome supply was plenty of Rye Flower, two hawsers, about a dozen coiles of Rope, eight or ten little kegs of pitch and tar, a small quantity of canvas, some twine, and a few sail needles. The coardage in particular was very usefull; it was full of tar and badly made, but exceeding strong for I dont recolect that any of it broke – and had we not met with this little supply should have been in the utmost distress, not having an hawser onboard of sufficient strength to heave up the anchor with, or other ropes to answer several purposses about the rigging; what we had left being now dry rotten.

We were informed by Capt. Smiloff that the Tchutskoi, a people who inhabit the eastern entrance of Siberia about Behring Straits, and the only Natives that remain unconquered by the Rusians, had this Summer voluntarily sent them a Large tribute of skins; which they were never able to exact by force, tho it had often been attempted. This was occasioned by our appearance upon their Coast, and they mistaking us for

---

1 An odd remark to make, a few days after burying Captain Clerke. He perhaps means a sickness contracted on board ship rather than a long-standing illness like tuberculosis; or he is suggesting scurvy.

Rusians, whom I suppose they imagined were come to carry on hostilities in order to bring them under Subjection; this accounts for their conduct when Capt Cook landed amongst them at the Bay of St. Lawrence a little to the Southwards of the Straits.

About a week before we sailed, twenty one head of oxen arrived here that had been colected and drove from a considerable distance, on purpose for us; they were of a modrate size, and in very good order, and proved a very great refreshment to us. Except a few for present use we killed the rest and salted them for sea.[1]

The Summer here is of a very short duration being little more than four months; for by October the Country began to have quite a wintry appearance, the Trees and Bushes having entirely lost their verdure and the weather grown cold; and I make no doubt but by the latter part of November or the beginning of December that the ground would be covered with Snow.

October 1779

---

1 Gilbert's journal from this point on was published as the concluding pages of Professor J. C. Beaglehole's edition of the journals of Captain James Cook (see preface) as the only document covering the last months of the voyage.

Chapter Six

THE JOURNEY HOME

Having completed our wood and water and got what Refreshments the place could afford, after a tedious stay of seven
weeks, on the 10th of October 1779 we sailed out of the Bay;
and having fine weather we surveyed the coast down to Cape
Lopatka; which is the southern extremity of Kamchatka and
lies in Lat: 50°N and Long: 155½°E. After this our intentions
was to explore the Kurelian Isles, but having a contrary wind
we saw not any, the Northermost of them that lies in sight
from Cape Lopatka; according to the Rusian's manuscript
charts, they are small and eighteen in number extending in a
chain SSW to the Islands of Iedso [Hokkaido], which likewise
we did not see, for the wind continuing westerly we could not
fetch near them; they are three in number of a modrate extent
and lie close to the NW of Japan.

From the incorectness of most old maps, Japan is generally   Japan
understood to be one large Island, when instead of that it is a
cluster of several; but three of them only are extensive the
others being very small. They lie close together and are
including the whole, almost the size of Great Britain.

About the 24th of October we made the NE point of Nipon
which is the principal of the Japanese Islands, and nearly as
large as the other two; this extremity lies in Lat: 40½°N and
Long: 141½°E. We stood within about two miles of the shore,
which is of a modrate height and to appearence very fertile,

being well cultivated and laid out into regular plantations presenting a most delightfull prospect. Having light breezes, we made but little progress along the coast which trends due South; the wind at last coming off Shore and a current setting to the eastward, we remained in sight of it only two days. We saw two Japanese vessels at a distance which bore down within two or three miles of us, but would not come any nearer; perceiving from the rate of their sailing that it would be in vain to chase them we therefore lay to, for some time; then fired a gun and hoisted our Colours, but all without effect for they stood away inshore. After three of four days the wind favouring us we made the Land about a degree and an half to the Southward of where we left it, having got within three or four Leagues of the shore; we had little winds and calms which prevented our standing to the Southward to survey the coast; and in two or three days we were carried out to Sea again, by the strength of the current.

November
1779

A few days afterwards, we saw the Land at the distance of about 12 Leagues and a great number of vessels close in shore; this was the S E extremity of the Island, lying in Latitude 35°N Long: 140°E, upon which there is a very large peaked mountain[1] almost equal in height to any we have seen. The Current seting round this point much stronger than before, drove us so far to the eastward that we found it in vain to attempt to make the Land again and the winter advancing we stood to the southward for China; we continued to pass by great quantities of pumice stone for several days which must come from adjacent volcano.

The greatest part of this passage was the most disagreeable we had ever experienced, having a continual gale of wind with very Severe Squalls, Thunder, Lightening and Rain and an extraordinary high sea; on the 14th of November we passed Sulpher Islands[2] laying in Lat: 25°N long; 140½°E; they are

1 Mt. Fujiyama, 12,389 feet.
2 'Sulpher Islands'; usually known as Volcano Islands. The Japanese name for Sulphur Island is Iwo Jima.

three in number, small barren and uninhabited; It was Capt
Gores intention, to have touched at two or three small Islands
called the Bashies[1] but by some means we missed them, as not
being quite certain of their situation.

A few days before our making the Coast, we fell in with a large
Reef; and it being then midnight and very dark, we did not preceive the sea breaking upon the Rocks till the ship had got within
the swell that rebounds from them, and had scarce time to wear
round and haul off. In the morning we bore away again and
stood close along the South point of the reef, which is called the
Pratas and lies in Lat: 22° 12′N Long: 116° 44′E; varies half a
degree west, it is of a circular form about six Leagues extent
and has a low sandy Isle on the west side, two or three miles
long, that seemingly a boat might land upon.

On the 30th of Nov. we made the Lama [Lema] Islands
which are a Range of Small ones, lying close to the Coast of
China. The Captains, now in complience with the orders of the
Admiralty, desired every Gentleman to deliver up to them their
Journals, charts, drawings and remarks of all kinds relative to
the Voyage and a diligent search was likewise made amongst
the sailors. The intent of this was to prevent any person
publishing an account of our discoveries, but such as their
Lordships should appoint, and when they thought proper. We
hauled round the Southernmost of the Lama Islands, and after
working up for three or four days came to an anchor in Macao
Road, to our inexpressable joy and satisfaction; having had no
intiligence from Europe for a space of three years, it being now
exactly that time since we left the Cape of Good Hope.

The next day we weighed and sailed into the Typa, which is a   December
well sheltered Harbour but rather shoal, having only 2½ and 3   1779
fathom water with an oozy bottom; it is large and formed by
four small high Islands, lying at the entrance of the River of
Canton, and is about 24 Leagues distant from that City. We lay
about four miles from Macoa, a small settlement belonging to

1 The Batan Islands, between Taiwan and the Philippines.

the Portuges; the citadel and other fortifications are in their possession, but the Town is cheifly inhabited by the Chinese, who will not permit them to go out of the small peninsula it is situated upon; it lies in Lat: 22° 10′N Long: 113° 48′E.

Macao
Harbour

IIere we heard of thc war with France, which was a very unexpected event to us, as in general we were of opinion that the Rebellion in America would have been quelled long before that time. The Chinese supplied us very plentifully with provisions of all kinds, but at a very dear rate; Capt King went up to Wampoo[2] where the India ships lie in a small Brigg belonging to one of our factors to procure Stores for us; and tho nine of them were there yet! we did not get so good a supply as we did at Kamchatka. Besides the usual duty we were employed in making breastworks and putting the ships into a state of defence; which had never before been an object to us. We made an exchange with one of our India ships, of a bower anchor, for six four pound pieces of Cannon; which compleated the Resolution to sixteen Guns, and the Discovery to 10. We sold the remainder of our fúrs to much greater advantage than at Kamchatka, the Chinese being very eager to purchase them and gave us from 50 to 70 Dollars a skin; that is from £11.5s to £15.15s for what we bought with only a hatchet or a saw.

January
1780

Two of the Resolutions people run away with their six oard cutter in the night and were not heard of afterwards. Having compleated our water, overhauld our rigging, caulked the ships sides, and after a very tedious and unnecessary stay of six weeks we sailed and stood to the Southwards.

On leaving the Land we had a very hard gale of wind and bad weather for eight days, till we made the Island of Pulocondore [Kondor Island] which is small and high, and covered with wood, and lies in Lat: 5° 39′ North Long: 106° 19′ East; we came to an anchor in an excellent Harbour on the NW side of it, where we moored the ships in six fathom water and staid for a week. There are a few Chinese Families upon this Island, of

2 He went to Canton, by way of Whampoa.

whom we purchased eight or ten Buffolos and killed them for
the use of the Ships Company. We caught plenty of Fish with
the seine; and cut a great quantity of wood, the place being very
convenient for that purpose. The shore at the head of the
Harbour is almost covered with mangroves, and monkies are
innumerable here; there is a small well of spring water on the
east side which we got a little from for present use.

On the 28 of January 1780 we sailed and after a passing thro
the Straights of Bankie [Banka] on the 12th of Feb., came to an
anchor in 26 fathom fine sand, off the SE side of Princes Island
in the straits of Sunda; which is generally alowed to be the
hotest and most unhealthy place in the world. The people here
are Malays of whom we purchased great plenty of fowls and
turtle at a modrate price; we compleated our water from a
standing pool which was but indifferent and having got what we
could, after a stay of five or six days, on the 18th of Feb. we
sailed for the Cape of Good Hope.

During this passage we were lucky in having fine weather
and in general favourable winds; till the last fortnight, when we
had light breezes, and calms; which are very unusual off the
Cape, where storms are mostly found to prevail. About two
days before our making the Land, we discovered six sail from the
masthead at a great distance, which we afterwards learned
were French ships of the Line that had been crusing there and
now going to the Mauritius; a fog coming on we saw them only
a few minuits – a little afterwards we fell in with a Large ship
that continued to hover about, at a distance, for two or three
days and then bore down to us. Which appearing rather
suspicious, we hove too and cleared for action. She passed
close to windward of us, with Imperial Colours, and stood on –
we likewise met with a small Eastindia Packet that was crusing
here with orders for their homeward bound fleet.

The Resolution having wrung the head of Her rudder very
much, was not able to turn up round the Cape to Table Bay;
therefore we was obliged to put into False Bay, which is sixteen

February
1780

March
1780

April
1780

miles distant over land, where we arrived on the 11th of April after a passage of eight weeks.

Here we heard of the war with Spain and received a proclamation of the King of France that had been issued out to all Commanders of their ships and vessels of war, forbidding them to intercept or molest us; it was found onboard one of their Frigates, taken by Admiral Keppels Fleet, and sent out by the Admiralty for us at our return. We found the Nassau and Southampton India ships lying here, being affraid to venture out on account of the French Fleet we had seen on the Coast. About ten days afterwards the Sybil Frigate arrived at Table Bay, and conveyed them Home.

May
1780

The carpenters of both ships were employed in making a new Rudder for the Resolution which was soon compleated, having refitted the ships and taken in a sufficient quantity of stores and provisions. After a tedious stay of a month, on the 9th of May we sailed for England and on the 12th lost sight of the Land. We saw three ships on our passage at different times, but they would not come near us.

August
1780

On the 9th of August we opened the Channel and I believe Capt Gore intended to go up it, had not the wind then shifted directly against us; upon which, we stood to the Northward for the western coast of Ireland with an intention to put into Galway; but the wind continueing steady from the Eastward, we were beating off the Coast for a week or ten days, without being able to make the Land, tho not above 30 Leagues from it. Therefore giving over all hopes of getting into Galway, we stood on to the Northward; and on the 21st of August made the western Islands of Scotland, which was the first land we saw since we left the Cape of Good Hope, after a very tedious passage of three months two weeks and three days; being the longest time we were out of sight of Land during the voyage.

The next day we got into Stromness Harbour in the Orkneys; but the reason of our putting in there when we had water enough onboard and a favourable wind to carry us round to the

River,[1] was known only to our Commander. It continued so for six Days afterwards, and then changed to the S.E. where it remained, and entirely prevented our Sailing; Capt King was sent away in a small vessel to Aberdeen with the Charts, Journals, etc to carry up to the Admiralty, and Mr Burney 1st Lieut. of the Resolution took the Command of the Discovery in his absence. Altho we procured every kind of refreshments, and met with very great friendship and hospitality from the Inhabitants, yet our stay at this place seemed exceeding tedious, and disagreeable; for we could get no more intiligence concerning our friends than if we had been at Otaheite.

After being detained here for a month, the wind at last came fair, and on the 20th of September we sailed from the Orkneys in company with several Merchant vessels. It was Capt Gore's intention to have gone up the Leith, but the wind blowing very fresh and directly down the Firth, we stood on along the Coast. Here two of the Resolutions people died; one of whom had then been two voyages of this kind and the other who was the sergeant of Marines had been three.

On the 30th of Sept we came to an anchor in Yarmouth Road, where each ship got onboard a new cable our own being too bad to proceed with. After two days we weighed and sailed up the River, and on the 7th October 1780 we lashed alongside the sheer hulk at Woolwich and the Resolution went up to Deptford. Both ships were immediately cleared and their crews paid their full wages, as a sixth rate, and set at liberty from the service except the Marines who were sent to their Division.

The Capts. Gore, and King were made post,[2] Mr. Burney and Mr Williamson masters and commanders; and every mate and midshipman that had served their time were made Lieutenants, and several of the men warrant officers.

Thus ended a long, tedious and disagreeable voyage, of four years, and three months, during which we lost only seven

1 The river Thames, the home port.
2 i.e. Post-Captains.

persons by sickness, who all belonged to the Resolution, and three by accident belonging to the Discovery, exclusive of those that were killed with our great and unfortunate Commander.

Finas.